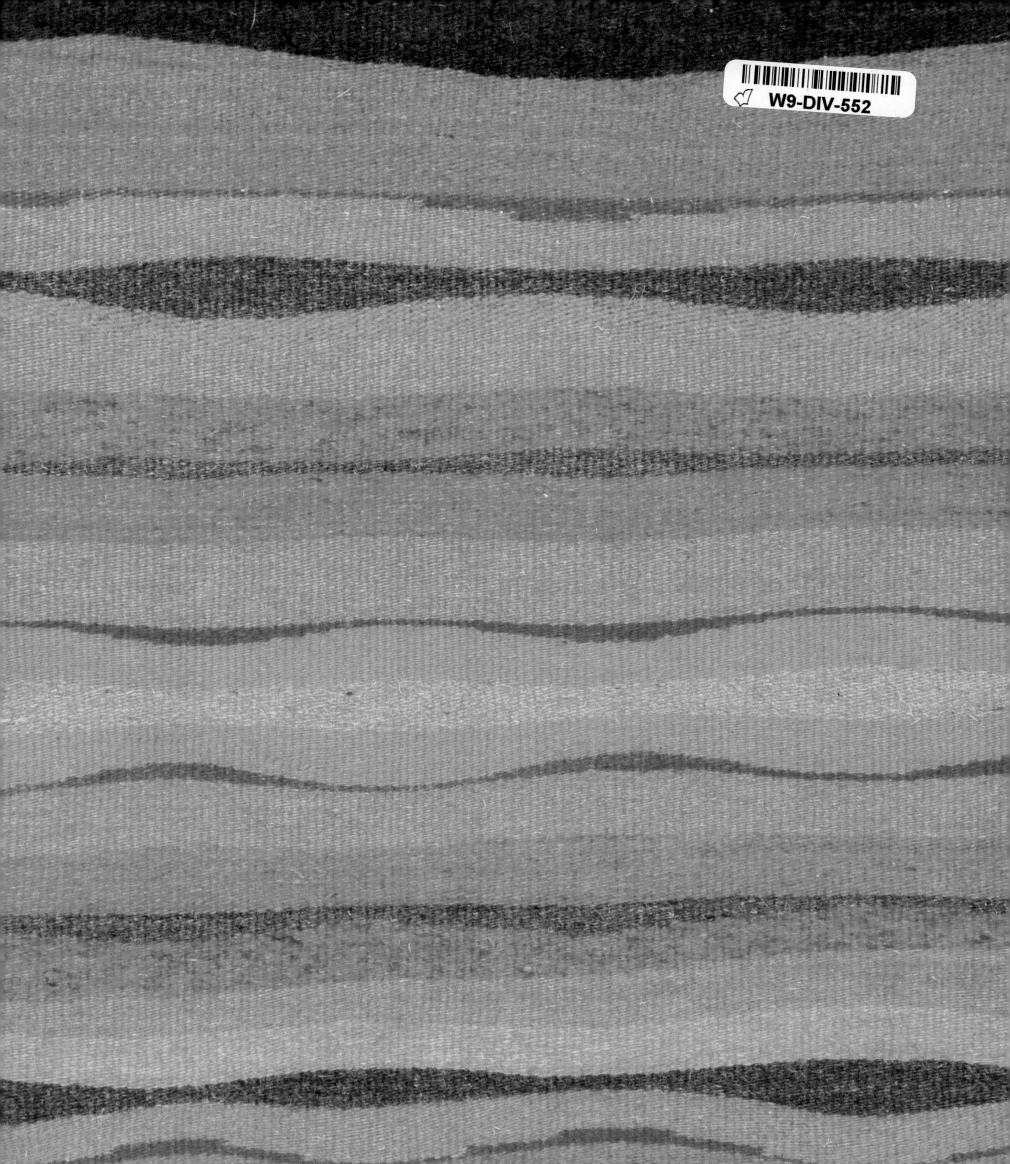

In This Way, Grandchild

Innocence in her curious eyes, a silent, purposeful child approaches her
Grandmother.

"*Bah-bah,* teach me to sing the clay."

Brushing silver-stranded hair from her intent face, pausing from her work,
she smiles.

"*Amuu, Tza Bah-bah,* come closer and listen. In this way, Grandchild, we
have been told to remember. . . "

In a voice slightly more than a whisper, she begins to pray.

*"Oh, Mother Clay and Great Creator, hear me. For this young one, my
Grandchild, I offer you my breath and once more ask for guidance.
From your sacred colored earth, I mix with water, move it in my hands
and shape these potteries. Bless them with fire, that the stories of all my
Mothers, all my Fathers, be remembered."*

Taking the child's small hands in hers, she traces the painted lines, lovingly.

You see, Grandchild, each shape, each design, has meaning in this
beautiful life, and Mother Clay helps us on our earthwalk. And for
those who came before us, who taught us, we must remember and
thank them, all of them. This sacred earth we live upon and share
with all its creatures—the rain that wets the earth, making things
grow—the sun and fire and its life-giving heat—the green plants for
our paints and brushes—the Grandmothers and Grandfathers who
showed the people—and you, *Tza Bah-Bah,* are part of all this. In
this way, Grandchild, we remember ..."

She picks up the large water jar decorated with many painted symbols,
turns it slowly in her ageless hands, and begins to sing:

"Wa-yo-ho-naaaaha, wha-y-ho-na-aahaa-a-yeh
... From over there, way over there
Rain clouds gather
And moving swiftly across broad horizons they come
Dark and heavy
They come dancing
Bringing sweet wet blessing to all my relations ...
Aahh-eloh-yah-aah, eloh-yah-aha-yeh-ehhhh!"

Harold Littlebird
Laguna/Santo Domingo poet and potter

AMERICAN INDIAN

GOLD ST.
PRESS

GOLD ST. PRESS

Published by Gold Street Press,
a division of Weldon Owen Inc.
415 Jackson Street
San Francisco, CA 94111
www.weldonowen.com

WELDON OWEN INC.

Executive Chairman, Weldon Owen Group John Owen
CEO and President Terry Newell
VP, Sales and New Business Development Amy Kaneko
Senior VP, International Sales Stuart Laurence
Director of Finance Mark Perrigo

VP and Publisher Roger Shaw
Executive Editor Mariah Bear
Project Editor Ashley Kircher
Associate Editor Lucie Parker
VP and Creative Director Gaye Allen
Art Director, Designer Marisa Kwek
Senior Designer Renée Myers
Production Director Chris Hemesath
Production Manager Michelle Duggan
Color Manager Teri Bell

A WELDON OWEN PRODUCTION
© 2008 Weldon Owen Inc.

ISBN: 978-1-934533-12-3

10 9 8 7 6 5 4 3 2 1

Printed by SNP Leefung in China.

Earth's Sacred Emblems

Quick and graceful deer, soaring eagle, slow yet steady turtle, hearty and sustaining acorn—these living things are all invested with value reflecting their practical and spiritual importance to American Indian communities over time. Though different tribes have diverse worldviews and cultural practices, many relate to the natural world in similar ways, and the emblems here represent the creatures and plants most ubiquitously meaningful in the nutritional, physical,

and spiritual life of Native communities, both historically and today. Their mutli-valenced power, evocative of the layers of the cosmic universe, is evident in their repeated appearance in tribal stories, clan motifs, arts traditions, songs, and ceremonies. Illustrations that depict those symbols are grouped according to the physical strata they inhabit, *below*. They are balanced around an abstract Zia Pueblo sun symbol, *left*, that represents well-being, abundance, and strength.

Found on Land

The great buffalo is considered a gift from the Creator, and his raw materials—from hide to bones to organs—long met many needs of daily life. Deerskins were used to make everything from tipis to clothing, and prized ivory elk teeth ornamented Plains dresses. First seen by the Crow around 1725, the horse radically changed life for Plains tribes, allowing them to cover greater distances more quickly. These highly venerated animals were stolen by brave warriors and traded among tribes. Nimble coyote features prominently in many tribal stories as a positive and negative cultural figure; present at the very beginning of time, he represents humanity's capacity to be both trickster and hero.

Glimpsed in Water

To peoples of the Arctic and Subarctic, whale hides, blubber, meat, and baleen make life in the harsh Northern climate possible. Killer whale, arcing from the water, is known as the guardian and ruler of the sea. On the seafloor live shellfish, from oysters to clams, which provided both food and lustrous inlay for jewelry and ceremonial objects. Salmon, char, halibut, and trout (among other fish) were eaten with great relish. For many tribes, salmon is of paramount nutritional and spiritual value, honored throughout the Pacific Northwest and Alaska. Tribes in the Southeast fashioned turtle shells into rattles for ritual dancing; to the Iroquois, turtle represents the earth, and sits ceremonially at the base of the celestial flowering tree.

Observed in Flight

Though some birds were consumed, their great spiritual power stems from the cosmic middle level they inhabit, where they share space with thunder and lightning, clouds, and rain. Their feathers, used in ceremonial adornment, are revered for their spiritual power. The eagle's broad wingspan assures his importance as one who brings prayers to the Creator. Raven—hero and rascal—is poised to steal the sun and bring light to the people, as he does in Alaska Native and Pacific Northwest creation stories. The Anasazi kept turkeys for ceremonial uses as early as A.D. 500, and wove their feathers into warm cloth. Wild duck is said to have helped the Ojibwe of the Great Lakes discover wild rice.

Grown from the Earth

Intertwined and grown together, the Three Sisters (corn, beans, and squash) provided the nutritional foundation for most tribes, and one or more of these plants still feature prominently in spiritual and ceremonial traditions. Corn, for example, was eaten, its husks woven into bags, its cobs used to polish pots, and its kernels ground into cornmeal to be left as a prayerful offering. Tobacco, the most sacred plant, was ritually grown and ceremonially smoked, sending prayers aloft to the Creator. Acorns, highly nutritious, were a rich and reliable harvest for California tribes; so important were they that tribes crafted beautiful woven baskets to process and cook the savory nut.

To Our Future

Sharing a meal has always been a way for American Indian people to create and sustain a mindful, emotional bond with one another. The gathering, preparation, and use of traditional foods, such as those described here, are distinctive to who we are as Native people. The act of preparing and sharing a meal with family, friends, or even strangers brings our souls together in a human connection. Native America celebrates human connections; it is a small window to our past, a collection of gifts devotedly preserved by our elders and documented by our young ones, so we can share in celebration with our future. This book is about the preservation of culture and regional family traditions.

Many of my first memories are of family and community celebrations that involved lots of food and organized chaos in the preparation of our meals. Today, three generations of our family gather annually at Wildflower Farm to partake of an annual four-day fall feast. Each year we light an extraordinary bonfire, enjoy midnight cooking, guitar playing and singing, and the fallen trees. We tell exaggerated stories and revel in kids, elders, laughter, and the familiar, traditional chaos of our meal preparation. Our family gatherings are casual and we all travel from distant and unique places to relax together. We share cooking techniques and recipes. And we always carefully prepare the sweet potato dish passed down from our beloved, but departed, Aunt Peggy—all with the silent awareness and appreciation of the affection, history, and family culture that binds us together with the past.

As I was the only daughter in a family of rambunctious boys, my Cherokee mother enlisted me to help her in the kitchen at an early age; of course I had the most important job—preparing the string beans that would complement our meal. Before mom would entrust me with the large basket of beans, she sat me on the sink and taught me her technique for bean snapping and string pulling. It was a fluid two-step process. Her technique required concentration, speed, and precision that kept me busy and out from under her feet. Now, as our family gathers to cook, I find that this unique family experience is a gateway to uninhibited conversations between fathers and sons, brothers and sisters, aunties and uncles, grandparents and grandchildren, mothers and their daughters.

As in many Native American families, everyone in my family has a favorite food specialty passed down from our family elders that is often prepared for family gatherings. My grandmother loved to make corn cakes and fried green tomatoes. My grandfather was known for his "surprise" stew and his willingness to share one of his many delicious pickled vegetables. My father has a special way of cooking the catfish that my brothers and I drag on shore, and my mother, the most adventuresome one in our family, often prepares my grandmother's tasty panfried rabbit. Personally, I take after my grandfather and I am known for my hearty winter stews and soups.

One of my great pleasures is to find the time to cook. I am an avid collector of cultural cookbooks. My cookbook collection is extensive and could certainly be categorized as a history in cultural preservation—I collect cookbooks that discuss and visually portray cultural regional cooking techniques and showcase traditional cooking methods with the presentation of food. I know the pages of this American Indian book will soon be well worn as a historical resource of traditional cooking and food preparation methods, and for its exploration of historical and contemporary arts, music, and other cultural practices. I appreciate the personal stories and photography contained throughout this book because it highlights the uniqueness of our people and the distinctiveness of our family traditions, and shares the regions and communities that are Native America.

To Our Future

Quanah Crossland Stamps
Commissioner, Administration for Native Americans

my father was an original allottee, born before Oklahoma statehood. As an elder, he was like many a survivor, maintaining our heritage and language during a time of incredible change. To honor this upbringing, I have always invested my time to ensure that the needs of elders in Native communities are being met. My efforts led to the founding in 1987 of the NSAIE, which extends support to people in need through programs that support their cultural identity.

The NSAIE strives to increase access to supportive services and programs that will allow American Indian and Alaska Native tribal elderly to stay in their homes, as respected members of their communities and keepers of their traditions. The proceeds we earn from this book, on behalf of the Knowledge Preservation Project, will be used to support programs and services for American Indian and Alaska Native elders, in the ways that are most culturally appropriate and socially necessary.

We believe that elders are the center of our communities and their wisdom is needed by the generations that follow. The knowledge they have shared with our project strengthens my commitment to the mission and goals of this organization. We hope you enjoy the stories and portraits presented in these pages, the extraordinary and beautiful images of our history, and the wisdom of our elders. We appreciate your support in sustaining our traditions.

Mvto, Thank You

Steve Wilson, Chairman
National Society for American Indian Elderly

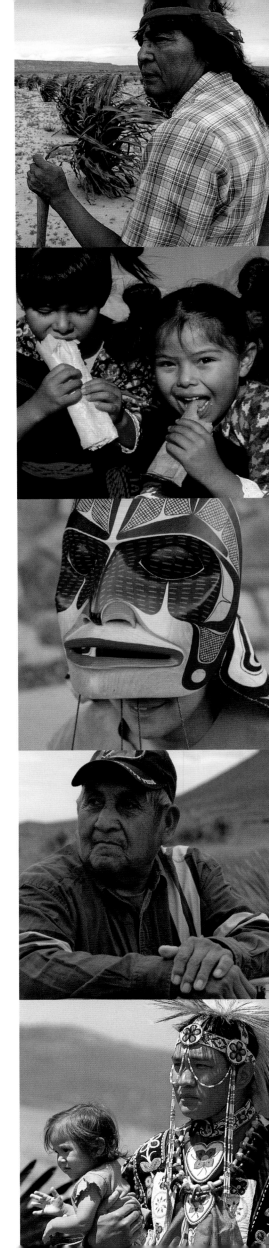

The Knowledge Preservation Project

Elders hold a special place in our culture: they are the keepers of wisdom. Revered for their knowledge and experience, they are sought after for their counsel, encouragement, and blessing. Today, we honor our elders through the Knowledge Preservation Project of the National Society for American Indian Elderly (NSAIE). This program, which collects and celebrates the indigenous knowledge bases of our elders throughout Indian Country, was created from a place of deep reverence, acknowledging our shared past and building toward a thriving future.

I grew up in the Muscogee (Creek) Nation of Oklahoma. Though poor, we were happy, and our parents provided for my family and for the many visitors and members of our extended family who passed through our door. My father told us to "be aware in the forest," since we spent so much time there fishing, hunting, and gathering wild fruits and berries. We fished for catfish and perch, or hunted squirrel and rabbits. We knew where to go to gather delicious wild blueberries, dewberries, blackberries, plums, and grapes, making sure we got there early in the season before my cousins, who also knew the best spots for picking. My times in the forest were special, and I would never give them up.

Back at the house, my older sister and I helped our mother can those foods in a hot and humid kitchen that lacked air conditioning. My mother always had a garden, full of traditional peas and beautiful purple and white corn. She would make *chetahoga*, or blue bread, from pea hulls. Once the children shelled the peas, my father would grind them into a fine flour. Every spring my mother bought one hundred chicks, which provided eggs and chicken for our many guests.

I was fortunate to learn firsthand from my elders, absorbing the stories and traditions of my tribe. My mother and father taught us many things. In fact,

Contents

To Our Future

Sharing a meal has always been a way for American Indian people to create and sustain a mindful, emotional bond with one another. The gathering, preparation, and use of traditional foods, such as those described here, are distinctive to who we are as Native people. The act of preparing and sharing a meal with family, friends, or even strangers brings our souls together in a human connection. Native America celebrates human connections; it is a small window to our past, a collection of gifts devotedly preserved by our elders and documented by our young ones, so we can share in celebration with our future. This book is about the preservation of culture and regional family traditions.

Many of my first memories are of family and community celebrations that involved lots of food and organized chaos in the preparation of our meals. Today, three generations of our family gather annually at Wildflower Farm to partake of an annual four-day fall feast. Each year we light an extraordinary bonfire, enjoy midnight cooking, guitar playing and singing, and the fallen trees. We tell exaggerated stories and revel in kids, elders, laughter, and the familiar, traditional chaos of our meal preparation. Our family gatherings are casual and we all travel from distant and unique places to relax together. We share cooking techniques and recipes. And we always carefully prepare the sweet potato dish passed down from our beloved, but departed, Aunt Peggy—all with the silent awareness and appreciation of the affection, history, and family culture that binds us together with the past.

As I was the only daughter in a family of rambunctious boys, my Cherokee mother enlisted me to help her in the kitchen at an early age; of course I had the most important job—preparing the string beans that would complement our meal. Before mom would entrust me with the large basket of beans, she sat me on the sink and taught me her technique for bean snapping and string pulling. It was a fluid two-step process. Her technique required concentration, speed, and precision that kept me busy and out from under her feet. Now, as our family gathers to cook, I find that this unique family experience is a gateway to uninhibited conversations between fathers and sons, brothers and sisters, aunties and uncles, grandparents and grandchildren, mothers and their daughters.

As in many Native American families, everyone in my family has a favorite food specialty passed down from our family elders that is often prepared for family gatherings. My grandmother loved to make corn cakes and fried green tomatoes. My grandfather was known for his "surprise" stew and his willingness to share one of his many delicious pickled vegetables. My father has a special way of cooking the catfish that my brothers and I drag on shore, and my mother, the most adventuresome one in our family, often prepares my grandmother's tasty panfried rabbit. Personally, I take after my grandfather and I am known for my hearty winter stews and soups.

One of my great pleasures is to find the time to cook. I am an avid collector of cultural cookbooks. My cookbook collection is extensive and could certainly be categorized as a history in cultural preservation—I collect cookbooks that discuss and visually portray cultural regional cooking techniques and showcase traditional cooking methods with the presentation of food. I know the pages of this American Indian book will soon be well worn as a historical resource of traditional cooking and food preparation methods, and for its exploration of historical and contemporary arts, music, and other cultural practices. I appreciate the personal stories and photography contained throughout this book because it highlights the uniqueness of our people and the distinctiveness of our family traditions, and shares the regions and communities that are Native America.

To Our Future

Quanah Crossland Stamps
Commissioner, Administration for Native Americans

my father was an original allottee, born before Oklahoma statehood. As an elder, he was like many a survivor, maintaining our heritage and language during a time of incredible change. To honor this upbringing, I have always invested my time to ensure that the needs of elders in Native communities are being met. My efforts led to the founding in 1987 of the NSAIE, which extends support to people in need through programs that support their cultural identity.

The NSAIE strives to increase access to supportive services and programs that will allow American Indian and Alaska Native tribal elderly to stay in their homes, as respected members of their communities and keepers of their traditions. The proceeds we earn from this book, on behalf of the Knowledge Preservation Project, will be used to support programs and services for American Indian and Alaska Native elders, in the ways that are most culturally appropriate and socially necessary.

We believe that elders are the center of our communities and their wisdom is needed by the generations that follow. The knowledge they have shared with our project strengthens my commitment to the mission and goals of this organization. We hope you enjoy the stories and portraits presented in these pages, the extraordinary and beautiful images of our history, and the wisdom of our elders. We appreciate your support in sustaining our traditions.

Mvto, Thank You

Steve Wilson, Chairman
National Society for American Indian Elderly

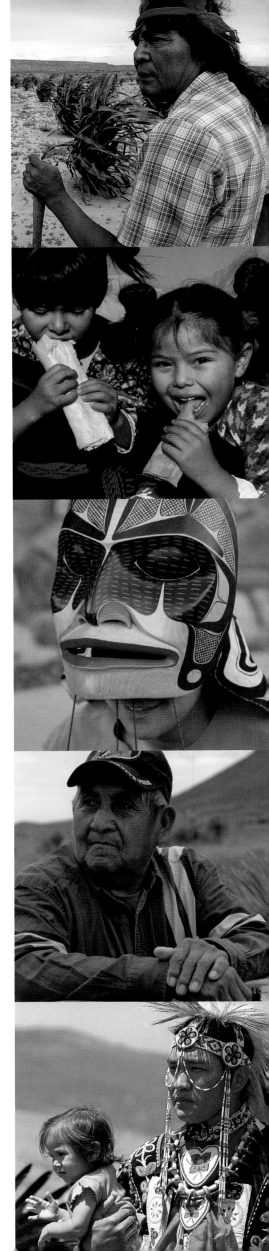

Harvests of Land and Sea

NEPHI CRAIG • WHITE MOUNTAIN APACHE/NAVAJO

"Steeped in tradition and simmering with knowledge, food is a vital affirmation of a people's lifeblood and culture, and the methods by which we procure it provide our communities with both spiritual and physical sustenance."

I remember the first time I saw my Navajo grandmother butcher a sheep—it was the day that she became a warrior to me. As a little boy, I had imagined butchers to be big white men who wore bloodstained white coats and wielded knives with their huge hands at the reservation supermarket. But one day, before a special ceremony, I watched in great anticipation as my grandmother—a kind, loving woman—marched outside to butcher a sheep in the traditional Navajo fashion. Before cutting its throat, she said a prayer to the sheep, thanking it for its life and the sustenance it was about to provide for our family. I stood still and listened to the prayer. My grandmother then carried out the task of skinning and quartering the animal with great respect and precision.

Experiences such as this have taught me to listen to the small yet profound voice that speaks to us through our foodways, echoing thousands of years of hunting and gathering technologies, but often overlooked in explorations of American Indian identity. Steeped in tradition and simmering with knowledge, food is a vital affirmation of a people's lifeblood and culture, and the methods by which we procure it provide our communities with both spiritual and physical sustenance. For this reason, foods serve as a delicate though powerful link between heaven and earth in the Native world.

Long before the arrival of Columbus or Coronado, the land and waters of North America offered up their natural abundance to the peoples who had the know-how and tenacity to use the earth's gifts. Before trains steamed west, hungry to cover new ground, buffalo (also called bison) roamed the central grasslands of North America. Moving in thunderous herds of millions, these sacred animals were hunted by dozens of American Indian tribes; they were either driven over cliffs in massive buffalo jumps or brought down with great precision using bows and arrows. Farther west, fishing provided a major food source for Native communities and served as a foundation for culture, spirituality, the clan system,

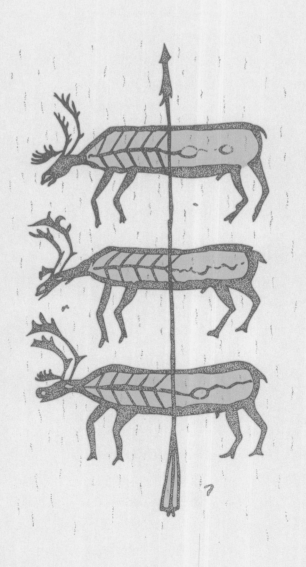

A clay Zuni water jar circa 1875, *above*, kept water cool. Three caribou speared by one long arrow are carefully incised on an undated Bering Sea bowl, *below*. The animals' presence on the bowl honors their souls.

and the economy. The rivers of Oregon and Washington once teemed with ten to sixteen million salmon and steelhead trout in their annual runs back to the springs of their birth. Lush forests produced berries, tobacco, and greens to supplement a diet of fish and sea life. In what would become California, acorns—laboriously gathered each autumn and processed into soup, mush, or bread—provided the nutritional basis for Natives throughout the region. By using the resources that the land provided, Native groups grew and prospered, developing spiritual rituals and arts traditions around food collection, storage, and preparation. For example, many tribes created pottery to store plants and meats for later consumption, and basketry to trap fish. Tribes such as the Tulalip of Washington celebrated the season's inaugural catch with a First Salmon Ceremony.

The staggered arrivals of white trappers, hunters, and pioneers from the East; Spanish colonists and missionaries from the South; and Russian settlers from the far North brought changes—both sudden and gradual, but rarely peaceful—to the continent's original inhabitants. In particular, the U.S. federal government began to forcibly relocate most tribal groups in the 1830s, causing dramatic upheaval to cultural customs, including foodways technologies. In unfortunate attempts to contain Native groups, reservations were often established in desolate areas ill-suited to hunting or agriculture. Tribes then had to rely on new foods available through military-issued rations, known wryly today as "commodz" foods. Ration staples included white flour, powdered milk, new varieties of beans, lard, and Spam—none of which are indigenous to a Native diet. Encouraged by the government, white sportsmen hunted the buffalo nearly to extinction in the 1870s, signaling that many traditional food-gathering methods were in danger of being lost.

Though this clash of cultures and policy hindered American Indian foodways, certain practices and culinary traditions were so culturally and spiritually vital that they have not only survived, but flourished. Today, for example, the Inupiaq and Yup'ik peoples of northern Alaska have resumed hunting the bowhead whale, with which they have a deeply spiritual connection. In 1977, ten villages formed the Alaska Eskimo Whaling Commission to regain their ancestral rights to harpoon the great sea mammal, upon whose bounty they have depended for millennia. When a whale has generously given itself to a hunter, the community celebrates with the *Nalukataq* feast and enjoys *muktuk*, or whale blubber and skin. They also engage in the age-old activity for which the celebration is named: tossing people in the air using a taut sealskin blanket. Because food is seen as a gift from the Creator, it inspires people to develop rituals and ceremonies that celebrate both the food gathering and the consumption of food.

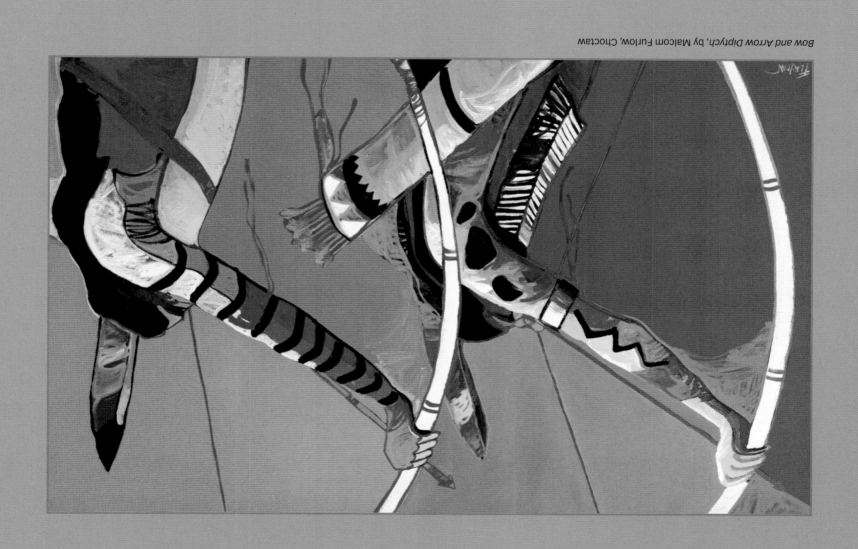

Bow and Arrow Diptych, by Malcom Furlow, Choctaw

As a White Mountain Apache/Navajo Native, my own experiences draw from those cultures' traditions, particularly the White Mountain Apache, since that is where I spent most of my formative years. Historically, the Apache were nomadic hunter-gatherers who roamed the land they called Apacheria, from the high forests of Arizona's White Mountain range to the arid Sonoran Desert of southern Arizona and Mexico, where wild game and vegetation were more frequently found. Apache groups mainly followed the seasons and game animals, though they also planted corn in the spring, returning months later to harvest the crop.

Today, like those of many other tribes around the country, Apache culinary traditions are recovering from reservation boundaries, commodz foods, and imposed hunting restrictions. The Apache are fortunate in that they have remained on and near their ancestral homelands; as a result, many foodways traditions such as hunting and gathering are still widely practiced. The agave plant and yucca fruit (known as the "Apache banana") are still ritually gathered for use in Apache ceremonies. Many varieties of corn are grown locally and enjoyed fresh, ground, dried, parched, or dehydrated in both daily and ceremonial uses. From black walnuts to venison to the rare but prized Apache trout, the bounties of the land are celebrated by today's tribal members, as by their ancestors before them. Certain sayings associated with food preparation and enjoyment are still used. For example, "If you eat the bone marrow from elk or deer, it will make you run fast."

Celebrating the catch of a whale, members of the community send a young girl sky-high in a *Nalukataq* feast in Nome, Alaska, *above.*

"*When a whale has generously given itself to a hunter, the community celebrates with the* Nalukataq *feast and enjoys* muktuk, *or whale blubber and skin.*"

A Catawba man and young boy take careful aim with their blowguns in this circa 1922 photo, *above*. Cane blowguns with their sharp darts were used to hunt birds and other small game.

The turn of the 21st century witnessed a gradual but important return to traditional food-gathering technologies, reintroduced by the tribes themselves. Hunting, whaling and fishing, ranching, and agriculture are all enjoying a resurgence, bringing spiritual, physical, and economic benefits to tribes. The Tohono O'odham nation of southern Arizona, for example, formed Tohono O'odham Community Action (TOCA), a grassroots organization dedicated to indigenous foodways and basketry, guided by tribal elders. Farmers with knowledge of traditional desert crops have developed growth systems for various strains of the Three Sisters (corn, beans, and squash).

Native foods are enjoying a culinary resurgence both within and outside of Indian Country, and their undisputed health benefits are an immediate reason for their rising popularity. Such foods work to combat diabetes, heart disease, and obesity in Native communities. Tepary beans, high in protein, help control diabetes through blood sugar regulation. Bison is a delicious lean protein alternative to other meats, and wild salmon is prized for its omega-3 fatty acids. Today, chefs pay top dollar for organically raised heirloom foods to support sustainable local agriculture, and Native professionals such as myself are increasing our efforts to promote the culinary benefits and inspirations of our heritage.

My mother taught me not to waste food, and always to bless each dish to show my appreciation. I ask that the food give us nourishment and strengthen our bodies; I express gratitude for the land we live on that provides us with these bounties. I believe that a return to Native foodways signifies a process of physical, spiritual, and social healing. As we remember and reinvigorate these processes, we invoke stories, art, ceremony, and prayer, and we celebrate community unity and tenacity. Through food and foodways, the past is honored and Native peoples are empowered as stewards of the earth.

In winter, the late afternoon sun casts long shadows. *Dried Geometry* by the Seneca artist G. Peter Jemison, *right*, depicts the Iroquois innovation of growing corn, beans, and squash together. Bare stalks and a trellis remind one of the past season's bounty.

The Three Sisters

Corn, beans, and squash, known as the Three Sisters, are of paramount importance to American Indian spirituality and nutrition. Originally cultivated by the Iroquois, the Three Sisters are produced through a system of companion growth, in which corn and bean plants share the same hole in the ground while squash blossoms utilize the shady spaces in between. This allows bean vines to climb the corn stalks and helps maximize nitrogen use, while squash leaves shade the soil and protect against animal pests and weeds. Nutritionally, the Three Sisters combined provide ample protein, carbohydrates, and vitamins, and are the basis of many traditional dishes, from succotashes to breads.

The Three Sisters were revered as special gifts from the Creator, and today they represent the physical and spiritual sustenance of life to many tribes. In fact, many Native histories mention the Sisters, who should be planted, eaten, and celebrated together. Feast dances still honor the life-giving qualities of one or all three of the crops.

Nature's Blessings

Tall and thriving, stalks of corn reach for the sky from Narragansett in Rhode Island to Navajo land in Arizona, *far and near left*. Calypso, Anasazi, lima, and Appaloosa bean varieties, *top*, are accompanied by colorful flint corn, *middle*, and deeply grooved winter squashes, *bottom*.

Gifts of the Sea

TRIBES OF ALASKA AND THE PACIFIC NORTHWEST

Salmon has been a wellspring of nourishment for the people of Alaska and the Pacific Northwest for centuries. Each spring, the fish return to freshwater to spawn, filling the bays and rivers and prompting celebration in the shore-lining towns. Tribal communities come together during annual salmon runs, when enough salmon is gathered to last the year.

The Yakama of the Columbia River pursue the flashing Chinook salmon, which can reach sixty pounds. Yakama fishermen employ traditional methods of hand-lining, dip-netting, *above*, and spearing, *left*. Salmon's firm, pink flesh is honored as part of the Yakama tribe's sacred First Food ritual, and the fish appears as a venerated character in many American Indian stories that stress respect for nature's bounty.

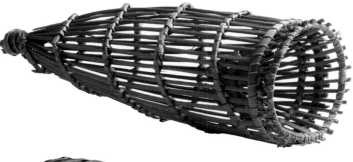

At the Stream's Mouth

Fish were a staple of many Native diets, and tribes with no connection to one another designed remarkably similar instruments to capture them. Handmade traps, weirs, and nets were used in the quick-running streams near tribal settlements. Though some families laid claim to particular stretches of water, others were fished communally.

Set against the current, the traps were conically shaped to draw in fish through a narrowing mouth; barbs on the inside made an escape impossible. Wide nets fanned out on either side to guide fish into the small opening. When the salmon ran upstream, the nets were easy to reposition. Once the traps were full of fish—salmon, trout, herring, flounder, or even eel—fishermen brought them ashore.

Delicacy of Form

Expert basket-weavers, the Pomo of California applied their mastery even to utilitarian fish traps. This exquisitely twined double basket with a funneled mouth, *left*, was woven from willow, and would have taken about a day to make. Sleek both in form and function, Siletz, Cherokee, Eskimo, and Powhatan traps, *above top to bottom*, show the breadth of raw materials and construction techniques used by tribes who fished many hundreds of miles apart. An Ingalik man of the Alaskan interior scoops ling fish from a large trap with a wooden scoop, *right*.

Careful Cultivation

SOUTHWESTERN TRIBES

Hopi Dry Farming

The late Eugene Sekaquaptewa tends his crops in the Eagle Clan cornfield below the Hopi pueblo of Old Oraibi, *above bottom and near right*. The Hopi are still revered as some of the best dry farmers in the world. The precious plots of land are passed down matrilineally; younger Hopi women take over care of the gardens from their grandmothers and aunts once the older women can no longer easily descend from their mesa homes.

The cultivation of crops did not come easily for tribes who carved out life in the arid deserts of the Southwest. Ingenious methods, including flood irrigation, were devised by the Anasazi to make the most of the infrequent rainfall. Dry farming, *left top*, and waffle irrigation systems, *right*, help present-day tribes of New Mexico and Arizona grow their crops, including the invaluable corn. In dry farming, seeds are planted at the mouths of gullies and streams, primed to catch water runoff during the short flood season. Waffle or grid gardening involves the careful construction of small mud walls around seedlings. These walls act as dams to ensure that hand-poured water is absorbed directly into root systems. Both farming practices entail a high level of perseverance and patience. The payoff, however, is great, as many crops are coaxed forth that would otherwise die: peaches, watermelon, and mint among them.

"A whale will not give itself to you unless there is a clean place for it to rest."

Mary Sage, Inupiaq

Whaling in the Northern Seas

ALASKA NATIVE TRIBES

Each spring the ice retreats and the great whales follow, streaming through the frigid waters of the Gulf of Alaska and the Bering Sea. Heeding this ancient cycle, whaling crews load their wood and seal-skin *umiak* boats, *left*, and seek bowhead, gray, beluga, humpback, and fin whales. Alaska Natives believe that whales allow themselves to be killed only when they are approached with respect. To this end, whaling gear is reverently repaired and ice cellars for storage are ceremonially cleaned and readied. Once killed, whales are towed in, *above*, and then butchered and shared among the community. Today, whaling techniques remain largely unchanged, although Native groups have had to fight for their right to hunt in their ancestral waters. Though rifles may replace harpoons, and snowmobiles tow *umiaks* to the sea, the bond between whales and those who hunt them remains unwavering.

Hunting the Great Buffalo

PLAINS TRIBES

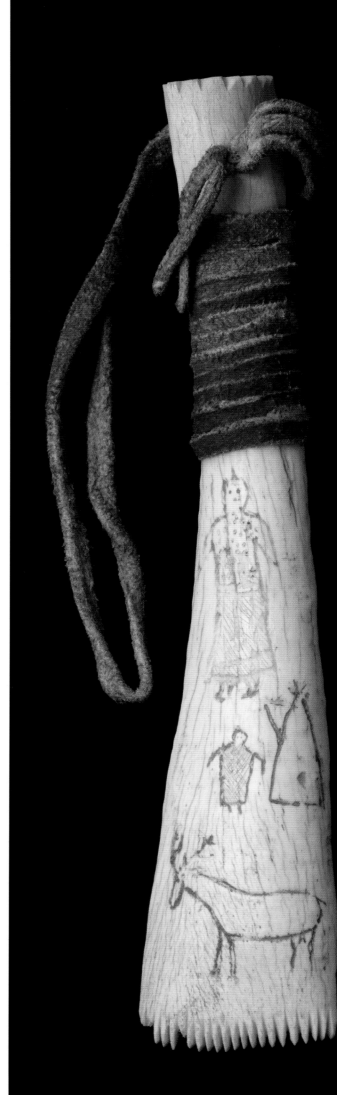

For Plains tribes, there is no creature more revered than the buffalo. Also known as bison, these shaggy animals once roamed the plains in the tens of millions before their near-extinction at the hands of white game hunters. Before the arrival of the horse in the 17th and 18th centuries, Native hunters engaged in a millennia-old practice of stalking buffalo on foot, driving large herds off steep cliffs called "buffalo jumps." This Piegan cliff jump, *far right*, shows the depths to which the animals would plummet. The advent of the horse meant buffalo could be more quickly (and more safely) tracked and then shot with bows and arrows or guns.

Once the buffalo fell, the women stepped in to prepare and dress the animals. A Bannock tribe hide-scraper, carved from elk bone and incised with human and animal figures, *near right*, was used to remove fat, muscle, and tissue from the valuable hide, *above*.

Herds of the Plains

The thunderous sound of running buffalo, *near left*, was synonymous with a tribe's survival. Because the buffalo was so essential to Native Plains life both practically and spiritually, sacred rituals led by medicine men nearly always preceded a hunt. These ceremonies involved prayers to the Creator for the buffalo's continued abundance, and expressions of thanks to buffalo that were shortly to give their lives so that the tribe might live and prosper. The strength of the buffalo was often depicted through song, dance, and story, and its likeness was painted on tipis, drums, and shields.

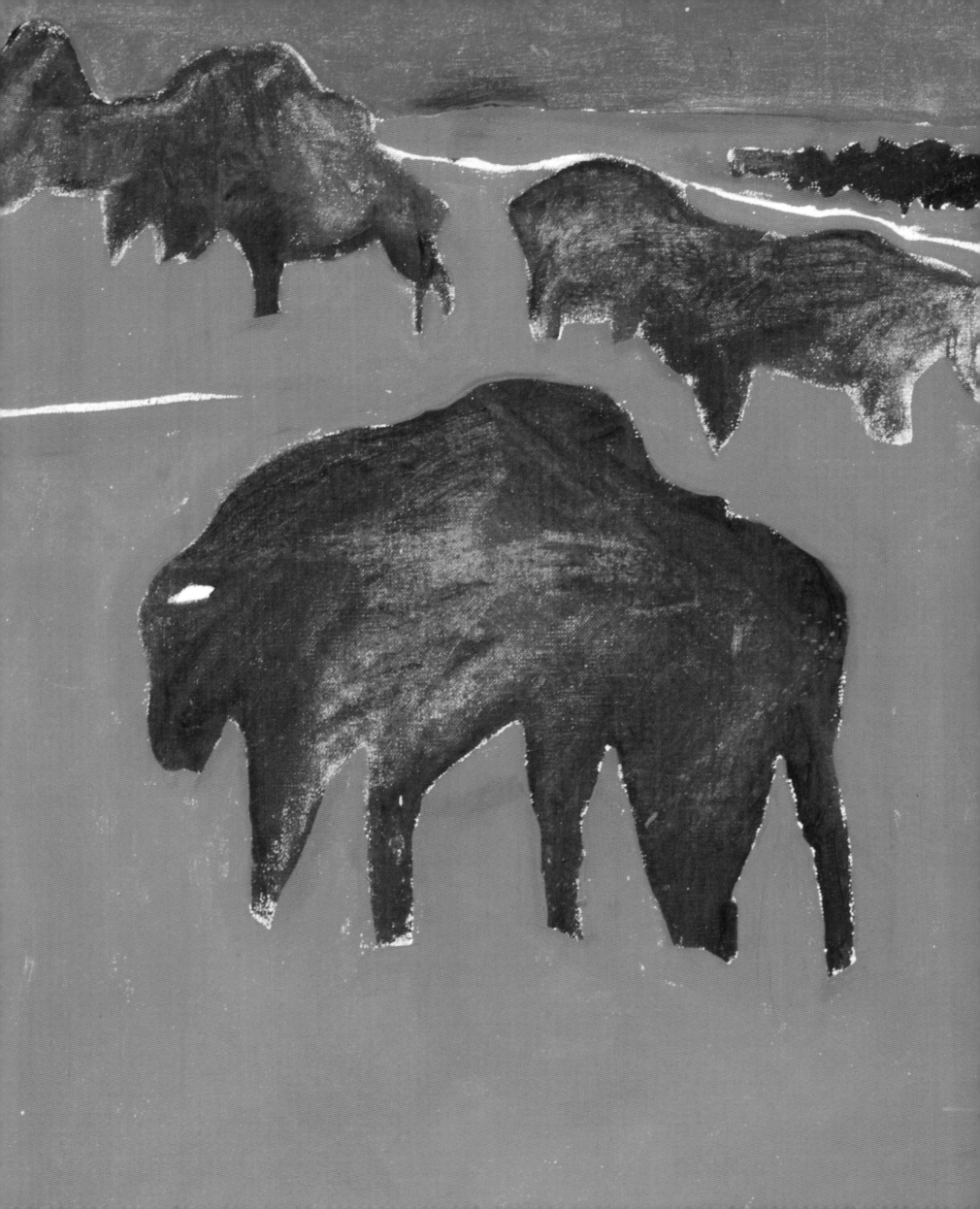

They Graze No More, by Bill Soza, Cahuilla/White Mountain Apache

Return to the Three Sisters

LORETTA BARRETT ODEN • POTAWATOMI

"Fishing and gigging frogs were hot summertime musts, and afterward we would devour huge watermelons and juicy, sweet cantaloupes."

I can think of no better beginning to the subject of Native cooking than from whence I came. Though my own tribe, the Citizen Potawatomi, are originally from the Great Lakes region, I grew up in Oklahoma—what I call the "melting pot of Indian Country." As a young girl, I was blessed to learn about food from my own mother, grandmothers, great-grandmothers, and aunts. Kitchens and gardens were where the women gathered to cook, talk, sing, and laugh. We collected wild greens including young pokeweed, which, once rid of its toxins through repeated boiling, was deliciously sautéed in bacon drippings. Come summer, the wild blackberries and strawberries would ripen and we would harvest the luscious first tomatoes. Fishing and gigging frogs were hot summertime musts, and afterward we would devour huge watermelons and juicy, sweet cantaloupes. As the days shortened, we would gather wild possum grapes and sand plums for rich jams and jellies, and we'd make bread from wild persimmons ripened by the first frost.

Though we enjoyed dishes created with these natural ingredients, we were also tethered to nontraditional foods distributed by the federal government. The Food Distribution Program assisted tribes removed from their homelands, doling out white flour, lard, powdered milk, chicken's eggs, cheese, and beans to those Natives who qualified. My own family's recipes reflected an adjustment to change. We ate huge pots of pinto beans with cornbread, perch or fried bass with crispy hushpuppies, and my mother's "goulash" made with ground beef and spiked with chile powder, which I now recreate with bison.

Of course, such cross-pollination of cuisines has occurred for generations. Travel and trade routes encouraged exchange among tribes, while explorers from Europe and Mexico introduced—and returned home with—delicacies and flavors that continue to shape global cuisine. Among Natives, culinary changes were also the result of the relocation of tribes from their traditional homelands and the use of non-Native cooking tools. Today, American Indian cuisine reflects the food

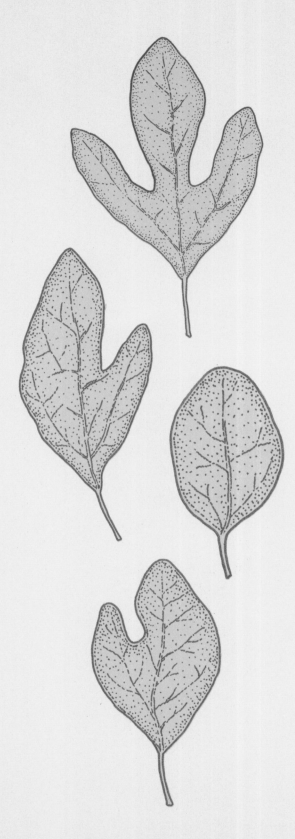

Distinctive oval and lobed leaves mark the fragrant sassafras tree, *above*, which grows from Maine to Florida. Once used medicinally by tribes, its use today is discouraged, as it can be toxic in large amounts.

practices of the Original People as passed down through the generations, including as wide a range of ingredients and tastes as the cook can imagine and create. My appreciation for Native dishes was informed by my own upbringing, as well as by these larger forces. As a professional chef, I use Native ingredients in ways that showcase their versatility, flavor, and simplicity. Whether serving up fresh oysters with a snakeroot mignonette or Native sunchokes tossed in a potato sauté, I honor the spirit with which the key ingredients were originally harvested or caught.

A tribe's "signature" dishes—from the everyday meal to a feast's centerpiece—represent its history and landscape. They tell intimate stories of the people that created them. As a chef and food historian, I feel that the dishes presented here provide dynamic insight into their tribes. They attest to the strength and elasticity of tradition, and are created with honor and served with pride.

The cypress groves and bayous of the southeastern United States—and in particular the humid regions of Louisiana—gave rise to aromatic stews and soups and inspired the first gumbo. Though the land was trained to support introduced vegetables such as okra, it was from the diverse coastline that most bounties were received. Crab, crawfish, alligator, and shrimp were consumed by the Houma, Chitimacha, Karankawa, Apalachee, and Choctaw. It was not until their adaptation of the sassafras tree leaf that the now-famous gumbo was born, later adopted (and adapted) by French Acadian/Cajun and Creole settlers. *Filé*, a spice made from the finely ground leaves of the indigenous sassafras tree, was originally used medicinally, until the tribes found that it could also flavor and thicken fragrant gumbo. Today, the Houma combine tomatoes, onions, and bell peppers, cook it to a slow, rich, red thickness, then add fresh gulf shrimp and *filé* powder. Though this particular meal is now commonly labeled a Cajun dish, its origins are firmly Native.

An arid expanse of desert and mountains, the Southwest remains a region deeply rooted in ancient tradition. American Indian groups still remain in their ancestral homelands, practicing food gathering and cooking traditions handed down over generations. In New Mexico, many of the nineteen pueblos still plant traditional gardens of corn, beans, and squash. Unlike the Iroquois of the Northeast, however, Pueblo Indians add to this triad green and red chiles. The amazingly beautiful colors of the corn and the long *ristras* of red chiles drying in the sun beg to be united in a delicious corn soup or a steaming bowl of *posole*. The process of making *posole* is an ancient one, derived from the Mexican dish of a similar name and nature. Dried corn is boiled with wood ashes or ground limestone (an ancient

process called nixtamalization) until the hull loosens and the corn blossoms into a soft, edible state. Accompanied by fresh oven bread baked in an outdoor mud *horno* and some spicy red chile paste, dishes such as pork *posole* or green chile stew are warm and hearty, as well as nutritionally rich.

Ubiquitous in Indian Country is one dish that comes under intense scrutiny: frybread. This seemingly innocuous dish was once made from whole wheat flour and fried in beef or pig fat. Later, the dish was made from white flour dough fried in lard, and became a favorite on the powwow circuit, served up with powdered sugar or honey, or piled high with beans and cheese in an "Indian taco." Today, many non-Natives believe it to be traditional American Indian food. But tasty as it may be, frybread—and nontraditional dishes like it—has wreaked havoc on the health of Native people. The ingredients found in these dishes have contributed to type 2 diabetes, lactose and gluten intolerances, heart disease, and other serious health problems. Frybread symbolizes both the innovation of the Native palate and the health threats faced by present and future generations of American Indians; however, it cannot be ignored as a mainstay treat of Indians across the country.

A Pueblo woman adjusts a hot loaf of oven bread baking in her outdoor mud *horno*, *above*. Each family builds its own *horno*, and its gently domed shape is a common sight in New Mexican towns and pueblos.

"*The amazingly beautiful colors of the corn and the long* ristras *of red chiles drying in the sun beg to be united in a delicious corn soup or a steaming bowl of* posole."

> **"***We lined a pan with maple leaves, then cleaned an enormous sturgeon egg sac, mashed the eggs, and placed the caviar—thousands of dollars' worth—onto the leaves.***"**

Brown and tan twined willow shoots and roots meet in geometric harmony in this Mono Paiute acorn-gathering basket, *above top*, as well as in this more intricately designed cooking basket, *above bottom*.

Before white flour found space in any Native pantry, acorns provided the main source of nutrition for many Californian tribes. Collected during special autumnal expeditions, acorns were shelled, sun-dried, and pounded into flour. Bitter tannic acids were leached out by rinsing and straining the flour through a woven basket or cloth. Resulting acorn meal was baked into bread or boiled into a mush using hot rocks and cooking baskets. Native women prided themselves on their ability to prepare the hot mush without burning their baskets. In fact, stories from the region say that a man seeking a hard-working wife might check the bottoms of her cooking baskets for any burn marks.

Natives of California also prepared dishes from the sea. Recently, I had the opportunity to prepare a feast with Yurok Elder Bertha Peters. As acorn meal cooked with hot stones and salmon smoked on sticks over an alderwood fire, we prepared sturgeon egg bread, an experience I will never forget. We lined a pan with maple leaves, then cleaned an enormous sturgeon egg sac, mashed the eggs, and placed the caviar—thousands of dollars' worth—onto the leaves. We placed maple leaves on top and cooked the whole pan in a slow oven until it reached the consistency of chewy bread. The rich flavors of caviar burst from each bite. The feast continued with acorn soup, fire-roasted salmon, dried sirfish, and smoked eel, accompanied by prayers, laughter, and stories.

Whether feast or everyday dish, each meal is prepared with generosity and intention, to be shared with family and stranger alike. The foodways of our People, though extremely diverse and often complex, are an integral aspect of our respective cultures. I often reflect on how much I have learned from my mother, grandmothers, and aunts, as the knowledge of food preparation—and with it the stories, prayers, histories, and lifeways of a people—are handed down to the next generation. Whether it is knowledge of when to plant crops, when to harvest acorns, or how to grind corn for Hopi *piki*, this knowledge must continue to be passed down. Once, when I was cooking with my granddaughter, Audrey Anna, she asked me, "How do you know how to make that, Granny?" At that moment I looked down at my own hands, and saw instead the busy hands of my mother and grandmothers, making the food as they themselves were taught so long ago. And so traditions continue, as we hand down the ways of our People.

A woven burden basket from the Arikara of North Dakota, *far right*, would have been worn while gathering food. The parfleche strap could be worn around the hips, neck, or forehead to free up hands for picking.

The Nourishment of All Life

ZUNI PUEBLO • NEW MEXICO

Salt is seasoning for ceremonial rites and culinary dishes. Navajos use it to celebrate an infant's first laugh, and Zunis once traveled with jars of salt and chile to flavor stews and meats. Salt was a valued trade item, and many tribes traveled great distances to gather deposits left on the shores of oceans and lakes. Such pilgrimages required purification of body and mind, and were not lightly undertaken. So sacred were these sites that, if warring tribes met there, they would put down their weapons in honor of the salt.

Zuni Salt Lake and *Ma'l Oyattsik'i*

She is known to the Zuni as *Ma'l Oyattsik'i*, Salt Woman, and dwells in the flats of Zuni Salt Lake, *left*. Each summer the water from these shallow spring-fed flats evaporates into heaping banks of shimmering white crystals. This salt, interpreted as Salt Woman's nourishing flesh, is gathered for ceremonial and domestic uses by Zuni, Hopi, Acoma, Laguna, and Apache tribal members who make respectful pilgrimages to the sacred lake.

Once, Salt Woman lived in a spring near the present-day Zuni village of Halona. Over time, however, the Zuni people failed to leave proper offerings when they collected salt, angering Salt Woman. She left the spring and created a trail to her new home, nearly fifty miles to the south. Though the Zuni people quickly followed and begged for her return, Salt Woman gently reminded them that if they continued to disrespect her gifts, she would leave for good, never to be found. And so to this day, all pilgrims who tread the well-worn paths to the holy spot leave offerings at her banks before they gather the precious salt.

Lakota *Wasna*

Derived from the Lakota *wa,* meaning "anything," and *sna,* meaning "ground up," *wasna* is a traditional Plains Indian food made from dried and shredded buffalo meat and dried berries, usually chokecherries. This high-energy food is rich in protein and vitamins, but its true asset is that it keeps indefinitely: preserved neatly in a hide parfleche, *wasna* made a perfect meal for many traveling Plains hunters through the ages, who roamed landscapes similar to the rugged plains and mountains of Wyoming's Teton Mountain Range, *right*. Even today, historians sometimes stumble upon caches of parfleche that contain *wasna* good enough to eat.

Traditional *wasna* is created in a buffalo-skin rawhide bowl by pounding equal amounts of dried berries and dried buffalo meat together with a hot stone until the mixture reaches the consistency of chewing tobacco. An addition of melted fat (either rendered from rich bone marrow or taken from around the buffalo's kidneys) allows the mixture to solidify as it cools. Finally, the mixture is rolled into balls and served or stored for later consumption. This traditional dish still finds a place at modern tables, though other varieties exist, including a sweet berry mixture and a vegetarian *wasna* made only with corn.

Grandfather, Great Spirit, once more behold me on Earth and lean to hear my feeble voice. You lived first, and you are older than all need, older than all prayer. All things belong to you—the two-legged, the four-legged, the wings of the air, and all green things that live.

Sioux Earth Prayer

Spice-Rubbed American Bison Tenderloin

LAKOTA • PLAINS

In a small, dry frying pan over medium heat, toast the cumin seeds, stirring constantly, until just fragrant, 2–3 minutes. Immediately transfer seeds to a plate and let cool, then grind in a spice mill or coffee grinder. In a small bowl, stir together the ground cumin, paprika, brown sugar, salt, ground red chile, black pepper, chipotle chile, and allspice, then set aside.

Prepare a medium-hot fire in an outdoor grill or heat a grill pan on the stove top to medium-high heat. Pour the spice mixture into a pie pan or onto a large, flat plate. Coat the steaks well with the spice mixture and shake off the excess. Place the spice-coated steaks on the grill rack or grill pan (if you are using a grill pan, reduce the heat to medium to prevent the spices from burning). Grill for 4–5 minutes on each side for rare to medium-rare meat.

Remove the meat from the grill and let it rest for several minutes. Slice the steaks thinly and serve warm.

Because it is so lean, bison should not be cooked past medium-rare or it will be tough and dry. Serve with braised chard or spinach, roasted potatoes, or spaghetti squash.

Serves 6

2 teaspoons cumin seeds

¼ cup sweet paprika

1 tablespoon golden brown sugar

1 tablespoon kosher, sea, or Apache salt

2 teaspoons pure ground red chile

1 teaspoon freshly ground black pepper

½ teaspoon ground chipotle chile

½ teaspoon ground allspice

Six 6–8 ounce bison (buffalo) tenderloin steaks

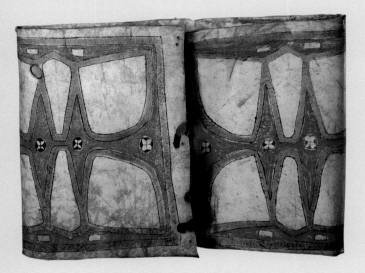

Traveling Bags of the West

For many tribes scattered across the country, from the Great Lakes to the Pacific's edge, portability was essential to maintaining a nomadic or seminomadic lifestyle. Over time, Natives developed technology for storing belongings in tight quarters and transporting items over great distances, on horses or by hand. Rawhide parfleche of the Great Plains and woven flat bags of the Columbia Plateau illustrate the skill with which tribes united practicality and tremendous beauty.

Derived from the French term *parer flèche* (to turn away arrows), durable, brightly decorated parfleche bags were used by Plains tribes to store clothing, food, and other goods. Used mainly from 1750 to 1880, parfleche were usually made from tanned, cut, and painted buffalo hide. Hunters on long journeys used them to store foods (such as pemmican) that could be preserved for long periods. Flat bags, also known as cornhusk bags and unique to the Columbia and Snake River Plateau, were made by Plateau-area women renowned for their skills in weaving. Cornhusk bags were once used to store dried herbs and root vegetables, but as white settlements began to encroach on digging areas, the bags were increasingly worn as purses and became sought-after trade items.

Parfleche

Sturdy and practical, parfleche cases are also works of startling beauty. Once the stretched rawhide was painted with natural dyes from plants and soils, a clear varnish—often cactus juice—sealed the rawhide and helped maintain the colorful patterning. Commonly found envelope shapes, such as those from Comanche, *left top*, and early Southern Plains tribes, *above bottom*, kept food dry. The Ponca trunk from Oklahoma, *right*, and the quilled Yankton or Nakota Sioux version, *left bottom*, are more unusual examples of parfleche. Blackfeet women carried their sewing materials in fringed parfleche cases, *above top*. Parfleche bags filled with dried meat were often given as gifts to visitors, which helps explain their ubiquity among most Plains tribes.

Cornhusk Bags

Considered a specialty of the Nez Perce, cornhusk bags are woven from hemp, elderberry, willow, or other bark without the help of a loom. Brightly colored decorative cords once came from beargrass or rye grass; beginning in the late 19th century, the slick inner sleeve was made from cornhusk. Later, these bags were fashioned with sophisticated false embroidery of colored wool or yarn. Different yet complementary colors and designs graced front and back, as shown in the turn-of-the-20th-century Nez Perce example, *right bottom*. The Paiute bag, *right top*, displays an interesting addition of hide handles. Diamond patterns like those on the Umatilla bag, *below*, feature prominently; exquisite details such as the four-legged creature, *left*, are not to be missed.

Three Sisters Sauté with Sage Pesto

PUEBLO NATIONS • SOUTHWEST

To toast the pine nuts, add them to a small, dry frying pan over medium heat, stirring constantly, until golden brown and fragrant, 2–3 minutes. Immediately transfer the nuts to a plate and let them cool completely.

To make the sage pesto, in a food processor or blender, combine the toasted pine nuts, sage, parsley, olive oil, garlic, lemon juice, and salt and process until smooth. Transfer to a bowl and set aside.

To roast the corn kernels, preheat the oven to 450°F. Spread the corn kernels on a rimmed baking sheet and roast until just golden brown, 3–5 minutes. Set aside.

In a large, nonstick frying pan, warm the oil over medium heat. Add the roasted corn kernels, zucchini and yellow squash cubes, beans, tomatoes, and a heaping tablespoon of the sage pesto. Cook, stirring often, until the squash is tender and the mixture is heated through, 5–8 minutes. Transfer the mixture to a large warmed serving bowl, garnish with sage leaves, and serve right away. Pass the remaining pesto at the table.

Serve this as a vegetarian entrée or as a side dish.

Serves 4

Sage Pesto

¼ cup pine nuts (piñon)

½ cup packed fresh sage leaves

¼ cup packed fresh flat-leaf parsley leaves

¼ cup olive oil

2 tablespoons minced garlic

4 teaspoons fresh lemon juice

½ teaspoon kosher or sea salt

Sauté

1 cup fresh corn kernels (from about 2 medium ears corn)

1 teaspoon vegetable oil or olive oil

1 medium zucchini, cut into small cubes

1 medium yellow squash, cut into small cubes

1 cup cooked or canned beans, such as Anasazi, Appaloosa, black, calypso, or lima

1 cup chopped fresh tomatoes

Fresh sage leaves for garnish

The Highly Prized Piñon

Slightly sweet and subtly nutty, the piñon, seed of the pine tree, *below top*, is an obvious accompaniment to any Three Sisters dish. Also known as pine nuts, piñon are harvested each fall throughout the Southwest and Great Basin region. Native gatherers use long willow branches to knock pinecones from trees like these in Capitol Reef National Park, Utah, *left*. The cones are heated over coals to release the stubborn nuts, which are then stripped of their soft brown shells, *below bottom*. Historically, tribes ate their fill of raw pine nuts, then roasted the rest of the protein- and oil-rich harvest to be stored and consumed throughout the winter. Mashed piñon "butter" was also spread on piping-hot corn cakes by the Navajo. Today, piñon may be best known to non-Native cooks as a main ingredient in pesto, though many tribes still celebrate the harvest of piñon. For example, the Walker River Paiute Tribe of Nevada holds the Pine Nut Festival each September, giving thanks for each year's harvest of this precious nut.

An Ancient Staple

OJIBWE • GREAT LAKES

Known to the people of the Great Lakes as *manoomin,* wild rice has been a valued and essential food source since tribes discovered it could be harvested. Packed with nutrients and easy to cook with, this flavorful "good grain" was considered a gift from the higher powers that guaranteed a rich harvest, and was both feast and offering during celebrations of thanksgiving.

During ricing season in early fall, men and women in canoes poled their way through the watery grass thickets, gathering ripened grain by knocking rice stalks over into a canoe with two thin, carved wooden "knockers," as demonstrated by this Ojibwe woman in 1941, *below.* Back on shore, rice was cleaned, dried and dehusked, and the chaff removed. This versatile rice cooks in a third the time of paddy rice, and may be added to soups and stews, fried into breakfast cakes, or parched into a popcorn-like treat and drizzled with maple syrup.

Processing *Manoomin*

A group of Chippewa break off husks by continually stirring the grain over a hot fire in large kettles, which also parches it, *left*. Potawatomi chef Loretta Oden expertly demonstrates how to remove the chaff from grain, *above top*. A quick flick of the wrist sends grain up in the air; any wind blows the unwanted chaff away, while the heavier rice falls back into the birchbark winnowing tray. At last, the grain is prepared and ready to be cooked, *above bottom*.

Water Brings Life

It is nearly impossible to overstate the importance of rain. For the Hopi, who live in an arid desert, rain means crops, which mean life. In Hopi creation stories, people emerge from the water and promise *Masaw*, the guardian of earth, to become good stewards of their new home. The Hopi artist Coochsiwukioma Delbridge Honanie depicts this relationship in his 1970 painting *Rain People and Planters*, *left*. In it, figures that may be *kachinas* move across a cornfield carrying items for planting. *Kachinas* are messengers who carry forth the prayers of the people to the forces in nature that bring rain. Honanie's colorful palette reinforces the celebratory significance of the event.

Great Lakes Grain

Wild grasses sway peacefully along the banks of Lake Superior, Minnesota, *right*. These elegant plants are a major source of nutrients to aquatic life and waterfowl, as well as to the Great Lakes tribes who have feasted on *manoomin* for generations. So valuable is this grain that the Ojibwe sprinkle tobacco on the lake's surface before beginning to gather it, signifying their appreciation and respect. Once harvested, *below bottom*, rice is often paired with other delicacies of the Great Lakes, such as sweet squash, *below top*.

It is said that the Ojibwe first discovered wild rice when a warrior named Nanaboozhoo ate a few grains that a duck dropped into his soup. Delighted with the taste, he followed the bird to a lake where the rice grew, and then shared news of his delicious findings with his tribe.

Squash Stuffed with Quinoa & Wild Rice

OJIBWE • GREAT LAKES

Preheat the oven to 350°F. Cook the wild rice according to the package directions until it is tender, but still slightly chewy. Drain if necessary and set aside. Cook the quinoa according to the package directions, taking care not to overcook it. Quickly drain and rinse with cold water in a cheesecloth-lined strainer until cool; set aside.

Meanwhile, arrange the squash halves cut-side down in a single layer in a baking dish or roasting pan. Bake until the squash are tender when pierced with a knife, 25–30 minutes.

To make the filling, in a large frying pan, warm the oil over medium-high heat. Add the celery and cook, stirring, until soft, 4–5 minutes. Add the green onions, cranberries, apricots, pecans, and sage and cook, stirring, until the ingredients are heated through, 4–5 minutes. Taste and adjust the seasonings.

Divide the filling mixture evenly among the squash halves. Serve right away.

You can prepare the dish in advance and keep it warm in a 200°F oven for up to 1 hour. For a festive and tasty presentation, serve the filling as a side dish and present it in a large seeded and partially baked pumpkin.

Serves 6

1 cup uncooked wild rice, preferably Ojibwe hand-gathered rice

1 cup uncooked quinoa

3 medium acorn squashes, about 1 pound each, halved and seeds removed

2 teaspoons vegetable or olive oil

½ cup celery, chopped

4 green onions (white and pale green parts), chopped

½ cup dried cranberries

⅓ cup dried apricots, chopped

⅓ cup chopped pecans or walnuts

1 teaspoon dried sage

Kosher salt to taste

The Gift of Hopi Gold

HOPI • ARIZONA

A delicate roll of paper-thin bread made from blue corn, *piki* has long been a staple of many Hopi ceremonies. The dish is so important that exterior kitchens are built to house the *piki*-making process, and the accoutrements used in its creation—such as stones, bowls, and trays—are precious heirlooms passed down for generations.

Preparing *piki* requires great patience; mastery of the process is a rite of passage for a young Hopi woman. Without assistance, she must create a generous repast of *piki* for her community, demonstrating her benevolence and the skills learned from her female elders. The seeds of this expertise are sowed early, when young girls learn to plant corn and raise the seedlings—much as they will someday raise their children. In the Hopi worldview, such reverence and knowledge perpetuates more than the tribe's traditions; it connects mother to daughter, and daughter to the land, in a spiritual bond that is as sustaining as the sacred food it creates.

"My grandmother always says to be happy when you're cooking. If you cook when you're angry, you feed only anger to your guests. Now I tell my daughters to have good thoughts while they cook, so that we too can fill our guests with happiness at feast time, and our prayers for rain will be answered."

Ruby Chimerica, Hopi

A Quick Hand's Work

Making *piki* is a lengthy but rewarding undertaking. First, blue corn is ground to a powder-fine consistency. A sprinkling of pumpkin, squash, or watermelon seeds cures the highly polished *piki* stone, which is placed over a cedar wood fire. The maker then creates the batter by mixing the flour with water and ashes from a saltbush plant. Once the stone is burning hot, she quickly spreads the mixture across the stone's surface with her fingers, forming a translucent parchment in moments, *left and right*. Multiple layers are pressed together to make the final product— a delicious, gray-green roll infused with distinctive flavor. Yellow and red corn *piki* are also enjoyed, *above*.

Readying for Winter

Yup'ik Elder Vera Spein uses a traditional curved *ulu* knife to cut small willow branches, *above top*, which are used to splay open freshly caught pink salmon, *above bottom*, so that the entire fish may dry equally. Each moment of the few weeks spent at fish camp must be utilized, for salmon caught during this important time must last an entire winter. Reliance on the fish is evidenced by its prominence in most Northwestern and Alaskan Native tribes' worldviews, arts, and songs.

A Year's Worth of Salmon

YUP'IK • ALASKA

Although tribes depended upon numerous types of fish for their diet, the salmon holds a powerful position. Prayers of thanksgiving were often spoken to the first caught salmon of the season, showing the respect given to the fish by tribes of the Pacific Northwest and Alaska.

Closer to the Arctic Circle, Yup'ik Elder Vera Spein prepares her husband's freshly caught salmon at their family fish camp just north of Kwethluk, Alaska. Each June, Vera employs techniques passed down by her mother, cutting fish on a diagonal and hanging them to dry over a wooden pole by their tails, *left*. Warm, sunny days are best, as too much moisture can ruin a whole summer's yield.

Other fillets are tended to in the smokehouse, *below*. Though the process varies between villages and even between families, some fish are smoked for only a few days, leaving them moist, while other thin cuts are smoked much longer. Smoked salmon is eaten on hunting trips, and is often the first item shared with visitors to an Alaskan home.

Fruit of the Wild Rose

Sweet and slightly tangy, rosehips have been plucked for use by tribes for hundreds of years wherever wild roses bloomed. Rosehips are the red buds left behind once the petals of the wild rose have fallen away, and are most flavorful after a light nip of frost, *below top and bottom*. High in vitamins C, E, and K, rosehips are used in curative teas by many tribes, combined with hibiscus, wild cherry, and spearmint. Rosehips are also reported to aid in relieving arthritic inflammation, sore throat, and irritations of the skin. For culinary preparation, larger rosehips are preferable, as they contain fewer seeds and more pulp, and are easier to cook with. Historically, the Crow made a special treat of pounded rosehips mixed with sugar and melted tallow, rolled into a ball and roasted on a stick. Today, rosehips are often used as a seasoning in soups and stews, made into jellies and jams, or served as an accent to game, or fish caught from rivers like this one in Oregon, *near right*.

Cedar-Planked Salmon with Rosehip Sauce

PACIFIC NORTHWEST TRIBES

Completely immerse the cedar planks in water for a minimum of 2 hours or up to overnight. Thorough saturation is required to steam-cook the salmon in the cedar vapors and avoid burning the planks.

For rosehip sauce, pour stock or broth into a heavy-bottomed saucepan and bring to a boil over high heat. Reduce heat to medium-low and simmer until the stock reduces by about one-third, about 15–20 minutes. Add rosehips, brown sugar, balsamic vinegar, orange zest and juice, and salt. Cook until the sauce reduces to 1½–2 cups and reaches the consistency of light syrup, 10–15 minutes. Set aside.

When you are ready to cook, drain the cedar planks and prepare a medium-hot fire in a covered gas or charcoal grill. (If using a charcoal grill, the coals should be covered with ash, but still glowing.) Spray the planks with nonstick cooking spray or brush lightly with oil, then sprinkle with salt. Rinse salmon, pat dry, and arrange fillets on the planks skin-side down. Keep at least an inch of space between each piece and at least 1 inch from the plank's edge. If using a gas grill, reduce heat to low. Close the grill cover. Cook the salmon, without turning, until just opaque in the center, about 15 minutes.

Arrange the salmon on a warmed platter. Reheat the rosehip sauce and drizzle over the salmon. Serve immediately.

Seedless rosehips are available at most health food stores. Find cedar planks at specialty food stores and mail order sources.

Serves 6

2–3 cedar planks

6 salmon steaks or individual fillets, 6–8 ounces each, preferably wild-caught Pacific salmon

Rosehip Sauce

4 cups vegetable stock or low-sodium vegetable broth

½ cup reconstituted seedless rosehips

2 tablespoons golden brown sugar

1 tablespoon balsamic vinegar

Zest and juice of ½ orange

Pinch of kosher or sea salt

Tidal Treasures

Tribes from both coasts savored the tender morsels of seafood plucked from coastal bays and inlets, *right*. Native families moved seasonally to the shore in order to harvest the sea's bounty; as with other food sources, nothing went to waste. The shells of clams, oysters, and scallops became spoons, tools, ornaments, and filler for rattles; even fish vertebrae were transformed into necklace beads. White or violet quahog clamshells were drilled and fashioned into strung cubits called *wampum,* a trading or monetary unit. Large sea-clam shells proved useful as serving plates and made strong farming hoes when tied to the ends of long wooden sticks.

Little mangrove or "coon" oysters were a favorite of tribes in the South. These sweet oysters were named after the raccoons that would snatch them from the roots of mangrove trees at low tide. On the West Coast, tiny and delicious Olympia oysters were the shellfish of choice among many tribes along Puget Sound, *below*.

"Every clambake must have a strong fire-keeper, or bake-master. My Uncle Byron was always assigned the duty, and was proud of the honor."

Dale Carson, Abenaki

A Traditional Clambake

The sweet meat and juices of the clam, *above top and bottom*, play a starring role in traditional clambakes. The genesis of today's clambake began with Northeastern tribes such as the Wampanoag, who dug fire pits, lined them with stones, and then built large fires, which they burned down until only super-heated rocks and glowing embers remained. Alternating layers of lobster, crab, unhusked corn, and seaweed were then baked and steamed over the heat, absorbing the flavorful juices of the dripping clams, which were laid on top beneath the final layer of seaweed. Today, chicken, potatoes, and vegetables often round out this simple, yet delicious, feast.

Inspired by Nature

Though nature could be bountiful, plentiful harvests and hunts were not assured. The ability to store and carry foodstuffs (from grain to oil) was important during times when sustenance could not be easily gathered. However, utilitarian concerns were not the only consideration when weaving or carving baskets, boxes, and bowls; like most Native storage containers and serving vessels, they were nearly always crafted with an eye for beauty. Though form closely followed function, an artisan's creativity was informed by the organic materials available. For example, the delicacy of Southeastern Chitimacha weaving fibers inspired the tightly woven, curvilinear basket shapes unique to the tribe. Similarly, cedar wood of the Northwest and Alaska, once cut and steamed into malleable planks, gave bentwood boxes their graceful lines.

Graceful Curves

The subtle colors of the earth suffuse this array of baskets and dishes from across Indian Country. A double-row snake design of plaited swamp cane winds its meandering way around a contemporary Chitimacha storage basket, *right top*, while a historic Chitimacha basket from the Louisiana region showcases a single-weave splint basketry style, *right bottom middle*. The large, elegant Choctaw carrying and storage basket, *below*, was made prior to 1880. Similar flowing lines imbue a red and black wooden Eskimo bowl, *right bottom left*, and a birchbark Penobscot Abnaki food dish, *right bottom right*. A Jemez Pueblo woman, circa 1930, washes grain in a yucca ring-basket at her village in New Mexico, *left*.

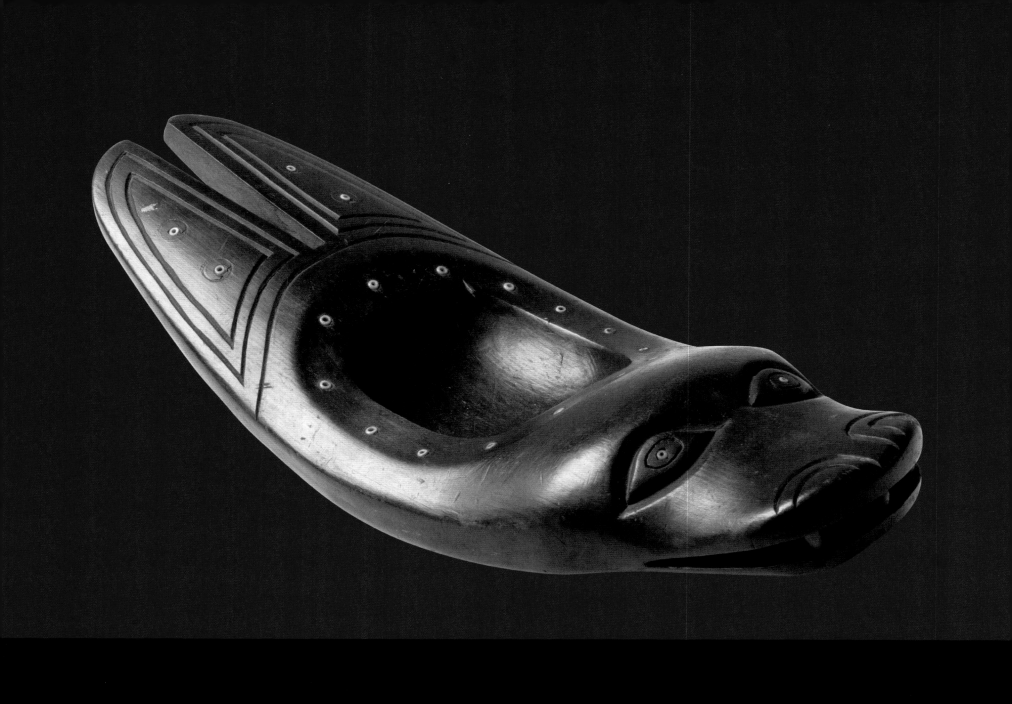
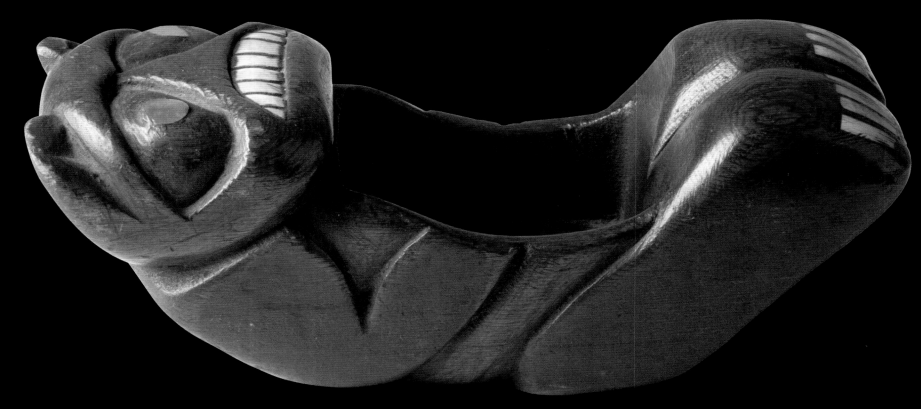

Gleaming Vessels

This zoomorphic grease dish, *left top*, attributed to a Northwestern coastal tribe, was probably used to serve seal or eulachon oil at a feast. Shell inlay emphasizes the sleek shape of this creature, most likely a seal. The deeper-basined Haida bowl, *left bottom*, features a bear whose eyes, teeth, and claws shine with shell inlay.

From One Perfect Plank

Sturdy, functional, and beautiful, bentwood boxes were hallmarks of the Tlingit, Haida, Tsimshian, and Bella Bella tribes along the Northwestern coast, and were used to store food, household, or ceremonial items. They were made, incredibly, from a single thin board of yellow or red cedar. Incised with grooves or kerfs at regular intervals, the board was steamed, then bent along the seams to form the four sides. The two ends were lashed together with cedar bark cord. A base and fitted lid completed the container. A red and black motif representing a mythical sea monster protects this dignified Tlingit food box, *above and right*, from Sitka, Alaska. Thirty-six rare shell opercula inlays decorate one side of the lid. Opercula were valued trade items; this box is unique for its extensive inlay.

Turkey with Cranberry-Piñon Sauce

ALGONQUIN • NORTHEAST

To prepare the turkey, place each medallion between 2 sheets of waxed paper. Using a meat pounder, lightly pound the turkey from the center outward until it is uniformly ¼- to ½-inch thick. Pour the flour into a pie pan and stir in 2 teaspoons each salt and pepper. Coat the medallions with the flour, shake off the excess, and set aside.

In a large frying pan over medium-high heat, add a thin layer of olive oil. When the oil shimmers, add several medallions. Cook, turning once, until golden on both sides and opaque in the center, about 2 minutes per side. Remove the turkey from the pan and drain on paper towels. Transfer to a platter and keep warm in the oven. Repeat with any remaining medallions, adding more oil as needed.

To make the sauce, drain the oil from the pan. Add the white wine and 1 cup of turkey stock. Bring to a boil over high heat, using a wooden spoon to scrape browned bits from the pan, until reduced to the consistency of heavy cream, 2–3 minutes. Add remaining 3 cups turkey stock, cranberries, currants, pine nuts, and a pinch of salt. Lower heat to medium-high until the sauce has reduced by half and has thickened, about 10 minutes. Yields about 3 cups of sauce.

To serve, place 3 medallions on each plate and ladle ¼ cup of warmed sauce over each serving. Pass the remaining sauce at the table.

Serve this dish with cornbread dressing. For a festive touch, garnish with minced fresh rosemary.

Serves 10

Turkey

30 turkey medallions, 2–3 ounces each

1–2 cups all-purpose flour

Salt and freshly ground pepper

Olive oil

Sauce

2 cups dry white wine, full-bodied turkey stock, or low-sodium chicken broth

4 cups full-bodied turkey stock or low-sodium chicken broth

2 cups dried cranberries

1 cup dried currants

½ cup pine nuts (piñon), toasted (see page 50)

Salt to taste

Tart Delight

Small white blooms herald the coming of bright red berries at the Cranberry Glades in West Virginia, *left*. Rich in potassium and vitamins A and C, cranberries, *below top*, have long been favored by Native tribes from Maine to Oregon. This hearty crop flourishes in the acidic soil of bogs and marshes, and many tribes harvested it each fall to use as a medicinal curative, dye, and food staple. Chief Pakimintzen of the Lenni Lenape served the berries at intertribal feasts to symbolize peace. Today, the Wampanoag of Martha's Vineyard maintain roughly 200 acres of wild cranberries. Each October on Cranberry Day, the community harvests the bogs by hand using traditional cranberry rakes. The berries are then consumed at the evening's celebratory feast. The meat of the wild turkey was traditionally paired with tart cranberries; Natives also made fans with turkey's lustrous, colorful feathers, *below*.

"I grew up on a ranch on the Blackfeet Reservation in Montana. My ancestors were buffalo hunters, but today we raise cattle. We always joke that now we're 'cow hunters.' My parents had ten kids, and so probably three or four times a year it was a family ritual to butcher a cow. We adapted the ways from the buffalo days of using every part of the animal, and my family would butcher, clean, and prepare food from all parts of the cow."

John Bird, Blackfeet

Times of Transition

Like the horse, cattle were introduced by European explorers in the 16th century; their impact has been immense. Cattle ranching eventually replaced the buffalo hunt as a relatively stable livelihood, suited to the confines of the reservation, *left*. With intention, as reiterated by Blackfeet Native John Bird, families value a cow's gifts of sustenance as they would the buffalo's.

Juniper-Braised Venison Shanks

POTAWATOMI • GREAT LAKES

Preheat the oven to 300°F. Pour the flour into a pie pan or large, flat plate. Coat the shanks well in the flour and shake off the excess. In a large heavy frying pan, warm the olive oil over medium-high heat. Add the flour-coated shanks and cook until well browned on all sides, 3–5 minutes per side, 10–15 minutes total. Using tongs, remove the shanks from the frying pan, drain on a rack or paper towels, and place them in a roasting pan in a single layer.

Drain most of the fat and oil from the frying pan, leaving just enough to cover the bottom, about 2 tablespoons. Add onions and celery and cook, stirring frequently, until soft, 4–5 minutes. Add the tomatoes with their juice, sage, and garlic, and cook, stirring, until blended, 3–4 minutes. Stir in juniper berries and 1 teaspoon salt. Pour tomato mixture over the shanks in the roasting pan, then add enough wine or stock so that the shanks are almost completely covered.

Seal the pan tightly with heavy-duty aluminum foil and place in the oven. Cook the shanks until they are fork tender, 6–8 hours. The sauce will cook down to a rich, dark, brick-red color.

Let the shanks cool in the sauce for about 10 minutes, then taste the sauce and adjust the seasonings. Divide the shanks among warmed serving plates, spoon the sauce over the top, and serve right away.

Serve with sage-flavored grits or roasted-garlic mashed potatoes.

Serves 6

¾ cup all-purpose flour

Six 3–4 inch meaty venison shanks

½ cup olive oil

2 medium yellow or white onions, chopped

4–5 stalks celery, chopped

2 cans (15 ounces each) chopped tomatoes with juice

¼ cup fresh sage leaves, chopped

3 tablespoons minced garlic

12–15 dried juniper berries, (depending on size and pungency), smashed or ground

1 teaspoon kosher or sea salt, plus salt to taste

4½–6 cups (1½–2 bottles/750 ml each) high-quality dry red wine or beef stock

Gitchi Manitouminon
k'manaaudjiko
K'gee gitchi zaway nimim
Mizukummikikway
Nadije minaudjee aumim
I gwi yen

Potawatomi prayer

Great Spirit, greetings.
For the many great gifts,
Mother Earth, for the life
you give all things,
thank you; it is good.

English translation

A Perfect Pairing

Herds of magnificent elk once roved the Great Lakes region, *left*. Hunted by the Potawatomi (who also hunted deer, moose, and bear), elk was renowned for the energy-boosting properties of its meat, which sometimes prompted weary hunters to eat the impressive creatures where they fell. Juniper berries, *above*, are often paired with elk meat and other game; the small berries lend a brisk, pine flavor to the lean, protein-rich fare.

Spice of Life

Vibrant rows of chile *ristras* dangle from awnings in New Mexico, *right and far right*. Hundreds of years ago, Southwestern tribes began assembling *ristras*—Spanish for "string"—to preserve the ever-popular pepper for the winter months. Now, *ristras* adorn entrances as signs of welcome and harbingers of good luck, and are still created in the traditional way. First, clusters of three mature red chiles each are braided along a string, then the colorful plait is laid out in the sun to dry. Later, peppers are ground into powder for use as a fiery seasoning, *below top*. Traditionally, *ristras* are strung to match the height of their weaver; this length is said to equal that person's chile-pepper consumption for the next year.

Southwestern Seasonings

Cultivated 9,000 years ago in North America, the chile pepper has long been a fast and fiery favorite among Southwestern tribes. Many varieties were planted, and tribes incorporated the chile's spirited flavor into signature dishes—both as a spice and as a whole fruit. One dish that incorporates the whole fruit is *posole,* a soup with Mexican origins. Composed largely of boiled corn and either pork or chicken, *posole* is punctuated by the spicy taste of red chile peppers and is served at celebratory occasions.

Rich in vitamin C and calcium, many chile varieties still grace tables all over the Southwest, from the standard Anaheim (often called the "New Mexico chile") to the tiny Chiltepin, which grows in the wild and is believed to be the most ancient form of the pepper. Green chiles are immature peppers harvested before turning a brilliant red, *far left bottom,* and are a bit milder than their mouth-searing relatives.

A Sumptuous Trio

The generous swell of a squash hull, a corn cob's tiny rows of kernels, and a handful of smooth-skinned, ovate beans—these three beautiful, highly nourishing foods make up the Three Sisters. First cultivated by the Iroquois in the fertile river valleys of the Northeast, *right*, squash, corn, and beans were revered as special gifts from the Creator. Enthusiasm for the harmonious grouping soon spread among other Eastern tribes, such as the Mohegan. Today, many tribes still honor the life-giving qualities of one or all three crops.

Even served up on its own, squash has always been a versatile component of the American Indian diet. Women of the Woodlands tribes would collect butternut squashes, *below top*, to bake whole—seasoning them with honey or maple syrup—or to boil into rich, fragrant soups. Pumpkins, too, were either baked, puréed into soups, or mashed like potatoes. Their tasty seeds were collected from the pumpkin hulls and roasted, *below bottom*.

Butternut Squash Soup

MOHEGAN • NORTHEAST

Place squash cubes in a large, heavy-bottomed saucepan and add cold water to cover the squash by 2 inches. Bring to boil over high heat. Reduce the heat to low and simmer the squash until it is fork tender, about 20 minutes. Drain well, reserving the cooking liquid.

Working in batches, purée the squash in a blender or food processor until smooth; take extra care during this step, as the squash is very hot and the purée could burn you. Return each batch of purée to the saucepan. While puréeing, if the mixture seems too thick, add a small amount of the reserved cooking liquid; the consistency of the soup should be thick, smooth, and creamy.

Preheat the oven to 350°F. Place the purée over medium-low heat and heat through, thinning it with additional cooking liquid if it gets too thick. Stir in a pinch of salt, taste, and adjust the seasonings. If you prefer a fresher, sweeter flavor, add honey to taste. Cover and keep warm until ready to serve.

To prepare the pumpkin seeds, pour them in a single layer on a rimmed baking sheet. Roast the seeds in the oven until just fragrant, 5–8 minutes, watching carefully so they do not burn.

To serve, ladle the soup into warmed soup bowls or hollowed, slightly baked acorn squash or baby pumpkin "bowls." Garnish with the chives or parsley and the roasted pumpkin seeds.

Serves 6

3 medium butternut squashes, about ½ pound each, peeled and cut into 2-inch cubes

Kosher salt to taste

1–2 tablespoons honey (optional)

½ cup raw, unsalted pumpkin seeds (pepitas)

⅓ cup minced fresh chives or flat-leaf parsley for garnish

From Sap to Syrup

OJIBWE • GREAT LAKES

Transforming the thin sap of the Northeast sugar maple into sweet syrup, sugar, and taffy was no easy task. Families converged annually at shared sugar bushes, or camps, where the sap was processed on-site. Collected sap was strained of impurities, then warmed and transferred from kettle to iron kettle until it boiled. If the sap boiled too quickly, a firm tap with a balsam bough into the boiling foam was enough to slow the process. Once the sap had reduced to thick syrup, it was poured into wooden kegs.

Remaining syrup went into the final "sugar kettle," where it continued to boil until it reached a bubbly, molasses-like consistency. This maple taffy was kept as a treat or poured in a wooden log-bowl, stirred vigorously until it granulated, *right*, then packed for storage or sale in large birchbark baskets. Maple syrup was a valuable commodity and was used to sweeten drinks and flavor savory dishes, as well as treat coughs, blindness, sore eyes, and other maladies.

A Communal Labor

Frosty, wintry nights produce the best sap, and families brave the late winter cold as soon as the first thaw guarantees the sap will run. Although modern appliances and materials such as metal sap buckets, *right*, assist today's sugaring process, birchbark buckets once caught the thin sap as it rushed down cedar splints pushed into the trunk, demonstrated by Mrs. John Mink at Mille Lacs, circa 1925, *above top*. Mary Bigwind and Maggie Skinaway of Mille Lacs, *left*, add to the pile of waterproof birchbark buckets they are making to tap the roughly five hundred trees claimed by each family. Before iron kettles were introduced, sap was boiled using hot rocks. Today's process remains arduous. From start to finish, maple sugaring requires enormous patience: twenty gallons of sap, boiled for an average of eight hours, yield roughly two quarts of syrup, or one glorious pound of golden maple sugar.

Maple Wild Rice Cake

WHITE EARTH OJIBWE • GREAT LAKES

Preheat the oven to 350°F. Grease and flour a 5-by-9-by-3-inch loaf pan.

In a bowl, stir together the flour, baking powder, salt, and cinnamon. Mix together the eggs, honey, maple syrup, oil, melted butter, and vanilla in another bowl. Add the liquid ingredients to the dry ingredients and use a large wooden spoon to mix the ingredients into a thick batter. Fold in the wild rice. Pour the batter into the prepared pan and bake until cake is golden brown on the top and a toothpick inserted into the center comes out clean, about 25 minutes.

In a bowl, mix together the walnuts, brown sugar, and butter. After the cake has baked for 25 minutes, use a spatula to spread the topping over the surface of the cake and bake until bubbly, about 10 more minutes. Cool the cake on a wire rack before serving.

Cut the cake into slices and serve.

Serves 6–8

Cake

1¼ cup all-purpose flour

2½ teaspoons baking powder

1 teaspoon salt

½ teaspoon cinnamon

3 eggs

1 cup honey

1 cup maple syrup, preferably Native Harvest

¼ cup olive or canola oil

¼ cup unsalted butter, melted

2 teaspoons vanilla extract

1¼ cups cooked wild rice, preferably Native Harvest (from White Earth Reservation)

Topping

½ cup walnuts

½ cup golden brown sugar

2 tablespoons unsalted butter

An Amber Harvest

Ojibwe cultural heroes Wenebojo and Manabush feature prominently in a story detailing how American Indians learned to produce maple syrup. One day, while standing under a gracious maple, *left*, Wenebojo was drenched with the sweet syrup raining down from the tree. Catching the golden liquid in a birchbark container proved so easy that Wenebojo decided such delicious fare should only be the just reward of hard work.

Nokomis, grandmother of Wenebojo, told him to show the people how to tap a maple tree by inserting a sliver of wood into its trunk and then draining the thick syrup into containers waiting beneath. Nokomis's other grandson, Manabush, reminded her, however, that without hard work, humans would never appreciate the treat. He climbed to the top of a maple tree and showered rain upon the leaves of the maple forest, greatly diluting the percentage of sugar in the sap and thinning it in the process. Today, in order to achieve the same amount of mouth-watering sweetness, a community must patiently harvest gallons of the maple sap and boil it down to a thick syrup, *below*.

Ready to Pick

Warm days signal the return of summer, and with this, the ripening of the berries. From the mouth-watering blueberries of Maine, *above top*, with their vibrantly red foliage, *right*, to the huckleberries of the Northwest and Alaskan coast, *above bottom*, berries held an important place in the pantheon of Native foods. In fact, many tribes named their summer moon cycles around berries: the Shawnee assigned July *Miini kiishthwa*, or Blackberry Moon, while the Haida noted that June occurred during *Canpasapa Wi*, the moon when the chokecherries are black. Prized berry patches were claimed by tribal clans, and during harvests, families came together to gather berries for the upcoming year. Berries were smashed into juices and jams, dried into patties, or combined with rich meats, providing bursts of sweetness all year long.

"At the end of August after the first frost we'd go and gather elderberries. And so those were used for medicines, for jams or jellies, or for a wine that they'd make for a medicine."

Pam James, Colville

Untitled, by Tony Abeyta, Navajo

Point of the Four Winds

DR. JANINE PEASE • CROW

"*Dried arnica flowers and wintergreen were reduced to a tincture and used to treat swelling and pain, and the Huron of the Northeast cured scurvy with annedda, the bark and needles of an evergreen.*"

A fever cooled by sassafras, a meditative glimpse of the Black Hills' rolling range, the powerful spirit vision of an eagle, or the anticipated resurgence of tadpoles each spring—these examples, both tangible and intangible, represent vital facets of the American Indian cosmos. They are also the key elements of medicine and healing, which are intricately interwoven within a general Native vision of harmony, spiritual power, and balance. The use of plants to cure physical and spiritual afflictions, sacred geography, vision quests and dreams, and cycles of life and death comprise the holistic American Indian worldview.

Perhaps the most widely known aspect of American Indian medicine is its innovative and well-honed use of plants as healing agents. Over time, tribes developed superior knowledge of plants and their many pharmacological benefits. These medicines have traveled around the world, and are still used in North America today as part of larger curing, or "medicining," ceremonies. Indians brewed a tea of poplar and willow tree bark to relieve headaches and minor pains; the active compound derived from these trees is closely related to that in aspirin. Black cohosh, a member of the buttercup family, was used to support women's health. Today, science recognizes the use of black cohosh as an alternative to estrogen replacement therapy. Healing ointments of balsam root were spread on flesh wounds, and witch hazel, made from *Hamamelis virginiana,* is an astringent still produced today. Dried arnica flowers and wintergreen were reduced to a tincture and used to treat swelling and pain, and the Huron of the Northeast cured scurvy with annedda, the bark and needles of an evergreen.

Herbal remedies were employed in various ways. Certain plants, such as sage, sweetgrass, cedar, and juniper, are still burned or "smudged" to purge negative emotions and purify people, places, and sacred tools. Similarly, tobacco—which is revered by nearly all tribes—is ritually smoked to send prayers heavenward. Sometimes tribes sang to activate the healing properties of the prepared

Settled inside the medicine lodge, an Arikara man contemplates a spread of pipes and herbs in this 1907 Edward Curtis photograph, *above*.

herbal medicine. The Seminole tribe of Florida, for example, sang prayers to the boiled ashes of trees; the ashes were then used to clean pollutants from the body of someone who gossiped. The words of the song referred to the otter, whose habit of frequent bathing kept its body clean. The knowledge of which plants to gather, when, and how, was passed down from elder to apprentice; their uses preserved through stories and belief systems.

Similarly, such belief systems preserve another key element of Native healing: the importance of physical place in providing a figurative and a symbolic foundation for tribal cosmology. For example, the Navajo believe in four subterranean worlds, stacked one on top of the other. On the level where humans live, four sacred mountains enclose the Navajo country: Big Sheep Peak in the north, Pelado Mountain in the east, Mount Taylor in the south, and the San Francisco Peaks to the west. Prominent mountains, rivers, and oceans have long been included in tribal histories as the places where life began or where worlds merge. This idea is essential to Native healing in that it defines the borders of the natural world; awareness of these boundaries reinforces the cosmic harmony so essential to both tribal and individual well-being.

The Pueblo peoples of New Mexico have a layered concept of sacred geography that is augmented through ceremonial practices. In the Pueblo cosmos, there are four underworlds and four upper worlds. The sacred worlds below are called *ochu*, meaning green, unripe, and sacred. The upper worlds, into which Pueblo people emerged, and where they live today, are named *shet'a*, meaning cooked, ripe, or hardened. This contrast of upper and lower is further symbolized in the Pueblo use of *kivas*, sacred underground ceremonial chambers. Reached by ladder at the bottom of a narrow hollow shaft, a *kiva* is understood as the actual place of emergence and is paramount in the Pueblo worldview; its use during preparations for ceremonial rites and dance-dramas of the masked spirits reinforces cosmic harmony. With each ascent up the ladder, participants reenact their people's mythic emergence from the sacred world into the world above, maintaining the strata of their unified cosmos.

This cosmos was also alive with spirit guardians in addition to a Supreme Being. In the American Indian worldview, all living beings have spirit guardians that act as guides and are revealed through dreams and visions; continued direct contact with them is essential to an individual's life path.

Traditionally, American Indians respect dreams as an influential part of a person's identity and spiritual life, especially in times of family or personal crisis and in times of change. Dreams once guided hunting parties and warriors on their

respective journeys. Additionally, young people on the cusp of adulthood would encounter their spirit guardians through dreams, and an elder's dream could inspire a name for a baby or child.

Spirit beings and guardians also appeared in visions. Most men and many women sought and received visions; however, there was a marked difference between the common visionary and the medicine man or woman. Medicine people had more than one spirit guardian. These spirits had the capacity to cure disease and even gave instructions on how to heal the patient. Certain animals or stones possessed spiritual qualities, and a medicine man or woman, guided by visions, could converse with them to seek their wisdom.

Some tribes held ceremonies to promote direct contact with the spirit world. Tribes of the Plains and the Northwest sought visions through the vision quest, an experience of fasting, sacrifice, and isolation in the wilderness, which is filled with lively spirit activity. Plains tribes expected their youths to participate in a three- to four-day vision quest, an experience of isolation and fasting. During this time, sacred powers—such as animal beings or natural phenomena—appeared to the vision seekers and often gave the youths their sacred names. At the end of the quest, the seeker reenacted the vision for tribal elders through stories, art, and dance. Through an elder's interpretation, the seeker might be given sacred songs and art, or even a new rite or ceremony, depending on the strength or clarity of the vision. So intense were vision quests and the appearance of sacred powers that people might assume aspects of their guardian spirits in their own personalities.

Patterns in the stars mattered greatly to many tribes. Images of the planet Venus, depicted as a four-pointed star, appear throughout ancient North America, as do spirals and star trails. These Anasazi petroglyphs, *above*, remain powerful celestial symbols.

"*Certain animals or stones possessed spiritual qualities, and a medicine man or woman, guided by visions, could converse with them to seek their wisdom.*"

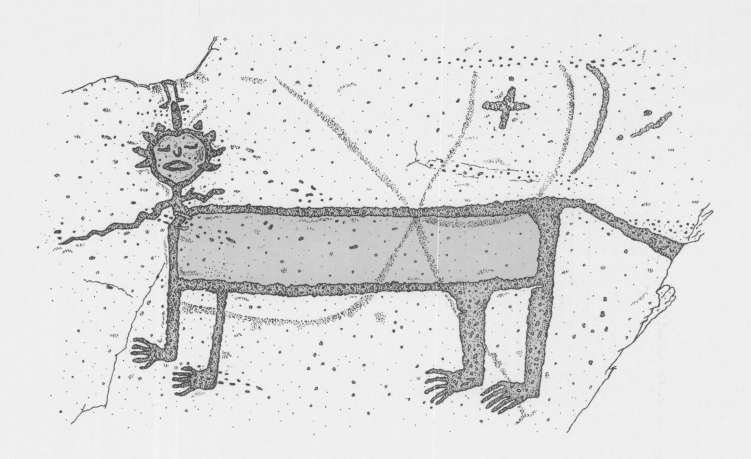

Sky and earth symbolism unite in this powerful medicine animal figure carved into a rock near Española, New Mexico, *above*. A mountain lion body supports a sun face with snake, while bear claws emerge from its feet.

"*Death is not an end, but the beginning of another revolution, echoing the orbits of the seasons and their stories. Even the words used to tell these stories lack past and future tenses, as most Native languages rest entirely in the present.*"

Stars keep watch over the the busy world below in *Rain of Life, Under the Stars* by Jemez Pueblo artist Felix Vigil, *right*. Strata of vivid colors show the interconnectedness of the earth's creatures.

For example, when Sioux women dreamed of Double Woman (a supernatural figure who appears as two women joined by a rope from which hangs a doll or a ball), they could expect to excel in the respected craft of quillwork.

The ultimate tenet of American Indian worldviews is a belief in the cyclical nature of life and death. Though death is inevitable, it is only a spoke in the larger wheel of life—an eternally recurring circle that is both personal and cosmic in nature. An individual's life cycles through a series of notable rituals that mark important changes: birth, puberty, initiation, and death. Death is not an end, but the beginning of another revolution, echoing the orbits of the seasons and their stories. Even the words used to tell these stories lack past and future tenses, as most Native languages rest entirely in the present.

In Crow history, it is said that when Old Man Coyote made the earth, he was helped by two ducks that dove down into the dark waters to bring forth roots and mud, which he used to make plants and hills. He then made men and women, and populated the land with animals. Old Man Coyote gave the earth its first drum and the dancing prairie chicken, and banished the angry bear to live alone in a far-off den. He bequeathed fire, weapons, language, tipis, and even war, so that the people might learn and sing victory songs.

This history of the world contains the kernels of Native worldview. The creation of the land and its plants, the people and their visions, and the endless cycles of the seasons ensure harmony and balance. The world, made whole, is a testament to—and foundation of—the omnipresence and relevance of Native methods of medicine and healing. The power of the smallest roots and the largest constellations restore and guide those who listen and observe.

Healing Herbs

Native medicine relies in large part on the effective healing properties of herbal remedies, as it has for thousands of years. To date, therapeutic uses have been documented for more than 24,000 plants. Native medicine developed from acute observation of animal behavior, as well as from trial and error. Plants were utilized from root to blossom, often chosen for the way their appearance—shape, color, smell, or taste—reflected a particular affliction. For example, purple iris petal poultices were applied to contusions because of their similarity to the bruise's violet hue.

Other plants treated spiritual ailments. Some were smoked or smudged, consumed, left as offerings to invoke visions, or used to begin a healing ceremony. Among these, tobacco is still revered by many tribes as the most sacred plant. Whether grown wild or cultivated, then dried, *below*, tobacco is smoked or chewed ritually. It is often used by the ill and elderly as a means of relaxation.

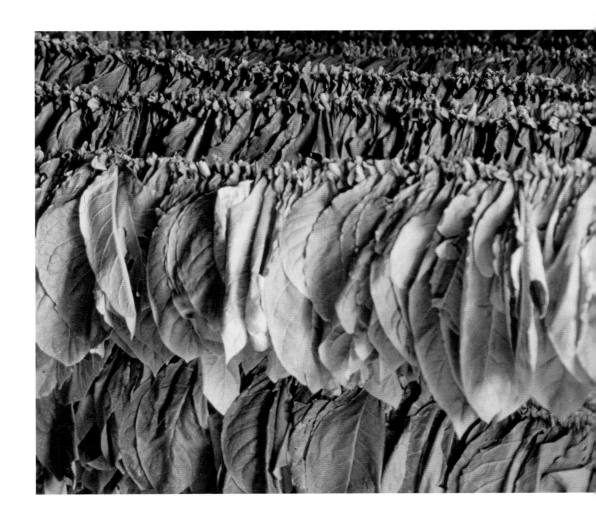

A Plant's Many Uses

Tobacco, cedar, sage, and sweetgrass are the four most sacred plants. Western red cedar, *above top*, is burned for purification and is used as an herbal steam to ease rheumatism. Shredded cedar bark may be woven into ceremonial regalia. Sage, *above middle*, like cedar, may be smoked or smudged. Its calming, aromatic incense is said to help drive away negative thoughts and spirits. Use of the root slows the bleeding of open wounds, and sage tea soothes sore and itchy skin. The fragrant, shiny blades of sweetgrass, *above bottom*, remind the Ojibwe of the hair of *Nokimis Akiin*—Grandmother Earth—and must always be braided before use. The three strands of the braid represent the body, mind, and spirit.

A Yakama woman wields a pointed digging stick to help her gather roots in Washington, *left*, and carries a distinctive bag woven especially to hold them. The Yakama had many feasts that celebrated the first foods of the season, including roots.

Root to Tip

Giant green leaves and bright red berries are protected
by the long, bristling thistles of the devil's club, *above top*.
Referred to as "Tlingit aspirin," its inner green bark is used
by Alaska Natives and some Northwest tribes to treat arthritis,
rheumatism, and even diabetes. Soft feathered yarrow leaves,
above middle, grow nearly everywhere, and are best known
for their ability to stop bleeding. Makah women nibbled the
raw leaves to induce easier labor. Runners chewed the hardy
roots of osha, *above bottom*, to increase endurance and to
treat respiratory illness. The plant is revered as "bear medicine"
for its powerful spiritual and physical healing properties.
Other plants such as rabbit tobacco, wild onion seed heads,
calamint, and St. John's wort, *right*, are dried for cooking
or for use in restorative teas and powders.

"Life for the Indian is one of harmony with nature and the things that surround him. The Indian tried to fit in with nature and to understand, not to conquer or rule. Life was a glorious thing, for great contentment comes with the feeling of friendship and kinship with the living things about you."

Luther Standing Bear, Lakota Sioux, 1931

The Peyote Sacrament

Peyote, a spineless cactus indigenous to northern Mexico and southern Texas, has been ritually consumed for more than 10,000 years. Dried "buttons," *above*, are believed to contain some of God's power, and are eaten during the Native American Church's Peyote Way ceremony. The Native American Church, with an estimated 500,000 members, must overcome certain obstacles to complete its peyote ceremonies. For example, nearly 90 percent of all peyote is grown in Mexico, but it is illegal to import it into the United States. Also, because peyote contains mescaline, its use by non-Natives is against the law; this leads some to misunderstand the powerful properties of the cactus and how it is used. Properly understood, peyote ceremonies are complex and deeply spiritual, a syncretic union of Native and Christian beliefs. Although the sunset-to-sunrise ceremony incorporates elements of both religions, it remains deeply rooted in Native healing traditions of prayer, song, and contemplation.

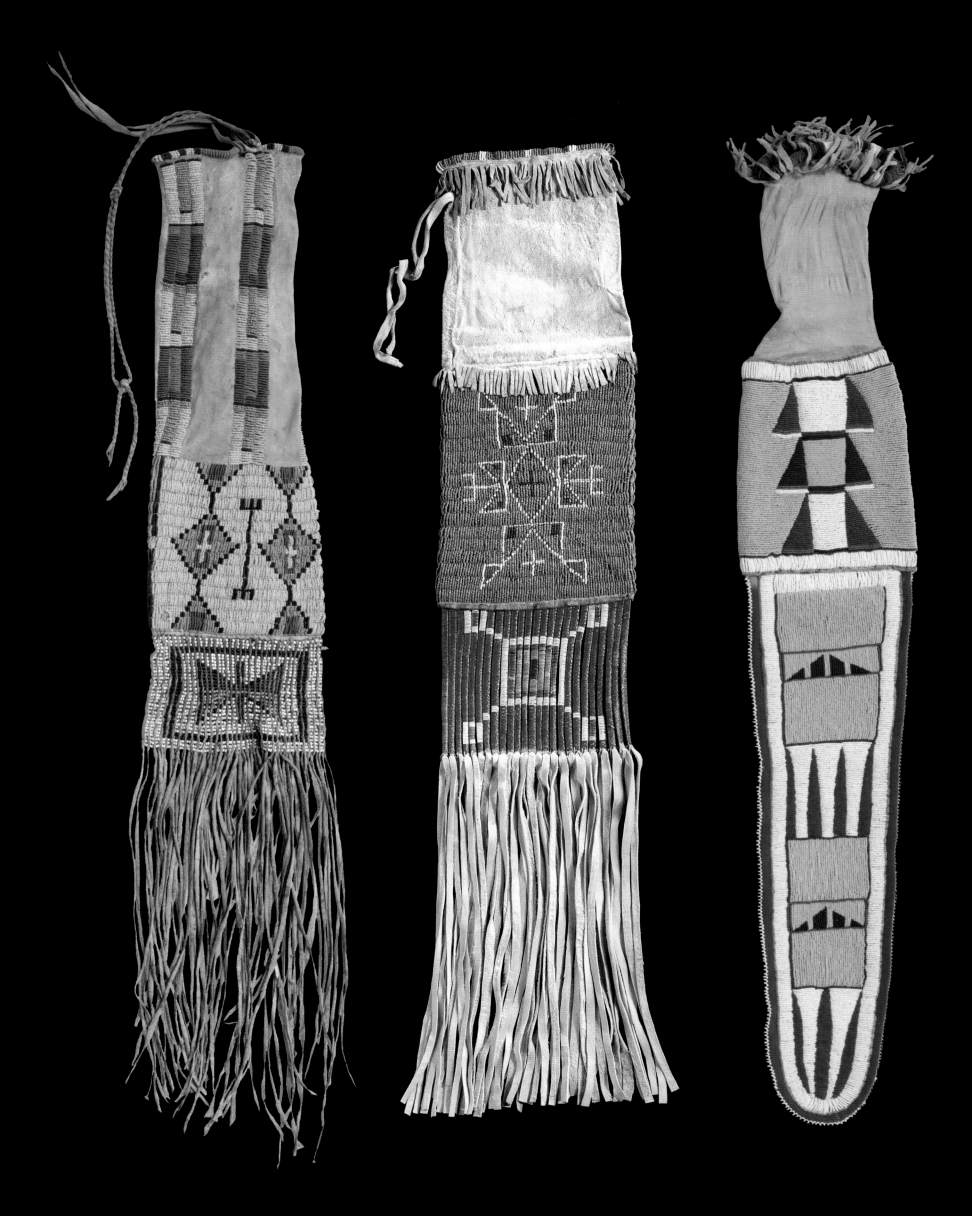

Beaded Pipe Bags of the Plains

Tobacco was many things to Plains tribes: a medium of exchange, an offering of respect, and an important presence in religious ceremonies, such as the sweat lodge. Tobacco pipes were the conduits that released sacred tobacco smoke, which was interpreted as a prayer drifting up to meet the Great Spirit. Pipes were rich in symbolic meaning; for example, treaties or vows made over pipes received the Creator's blessing and were thus rendered unbreakable. To many Plains tribes today, the sacred pipe represents the important relationships among the spirit world, the earth and sky, and all living beings. The pipe also symbolizes the creation of the universe, for the bowl represents the woman and the stem the man; joined together, they make the world whole.

Though medicine pipes were smoked primarily by men, the decoration of beautiful pipe bags was the creative domain of a tribe's industrious women. The artistry of such bags reflected the importance of what they stored. In fact, many creation myths feature a pipe bag that holds animals and birds to populate the earth. Tobacco was stored at the bottom of the bag in a smaller pouch, with the pipe bowl laid on top, facing up.

Protecting the Sacred Smoke

Most Plains pipe bags were a combination of animal hide (usually buckskin), glass trade beads, and quillwork, with a drawstring closure. Cheyenne, Oglala Sioux, Crow, Arikara, and Sioux examples, *left to right*, display variations on a theme. The Arikara pipe bag from North Dakota is unusual for its use of an entire skunk pelt. Bold colors and complex geometric shapes take center stage on the Oglala Sioux, Crow, and Sioux beaded pipe bags, while the Cheyenne bag displays long fringe and vertical strips of color blocking.

"Everything in existence has a consciousness, whether it's a pebble, a blade of grass, or a drop of water. Plants we regard as people, and so when we go to a plant, we ask it permission because it has awareness. It's appropriate to go to it and say, 'We ask your permission to take you; we're going to use you for something good, so that we may have good health. We also pray that your people will be replenished.' And then we leave something behind in exchange. For us in the North, where tobacco is our medium of exchange and respect, then it's tobacco that we leave. In the Southwest, cornmeal is their Bible."

Butch Artichoker, Oglala Sioux spiritual advisor

Bear's Lodge

Just as animals and plants are endowed with a sacred capacity, place also assumes the mantle of great spiritual importance. To the Sioux, for example, the Black Hills are "the heart of everything that is." Nearby in Wyoming, Devil's Tower, *left*, looms over the rippling plains. Also known as *Mato Tipi*, or Bear's Lodge, the ancient volcanic rock features prominently in the stories of many tribes. Through many variations, they recount that seven sisters, fleeing the jaws of a hungry bear, scaled the tall rock and then ascended to the sky to live forever as a constellation. The rock still displays the long vertical claw marks of the angry bear. Today, tribes journey to Bear's Lodge to conduct summer religious rituals, including vision quests, pipe ceremonies, and Sun Dances.

Sacred Seeds

The Tobacco Society of the Crow honored the tribe's most sacred plant. Members of the society prepared and planted tobacco seeds in areas determined by the dreams of powerful members, *above*; dancing and feasting followed.

Restoring Balance

HUPA • CALIFORNIA

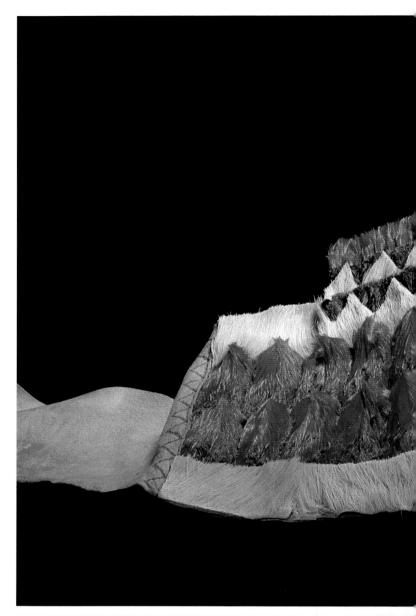

Scarlet-feathered woodpecker scalps stand at attention atop the heads of Jump Dance participants, *above*. The striking headdresses are a visual hallmark of the Hupa Jump Dance. This dance and the Brush and White Deerskin Dances comprise the Hupa tribe's World Renewal Ceremonies, which work to restore harmonious balance and defend against sickness and disaster. The Jump Dance stems in part from the Hupa creation story, in which a dark, disease-riddled cloud was driven away through a ten-day series of elaborate songs and dances as mandated by *Yimantuwinyai*, the main Hupa spirit. When the cloud finally disappeared, blessed rain cleansed the earth, signifying a disaster averted.

So influential was this Jump Dance ritual that all ten days were reenacted every other spring. Men strutted in pecking imitation of the great woodpecker, surrounded by women and singers who maintained the song's rhythm. The neighboring Karuk and Yurok tribes in Northern California performed similar dances.

Accoutrement of the Dance

All members of the community donned gorgeous regalia when they participated in the Jump Dance. Wealth indicated high social status, and prosperous tribal members provided elaborate dancing attire, such as this exquisite headdress made from white deer belly, red woodpecker and blue jay scalps, and yew wood, *above*. The headdresses were worn by dancers known as "middlemen." These dancers, surrounded by the singers, also carried sacred vessels known as jump baskets. These long, woven baskets were begun by women, then finished and decorated by the men; they were so important they were considered the symbol of the Hupa family. This circa 1900 jump basket is woven from beargrass and conifer root, and is decorated with feathers of the flicker, *left*. A middleman also wore a deerskin robe as a kilt, as well as any shells or beadwork he possessed.

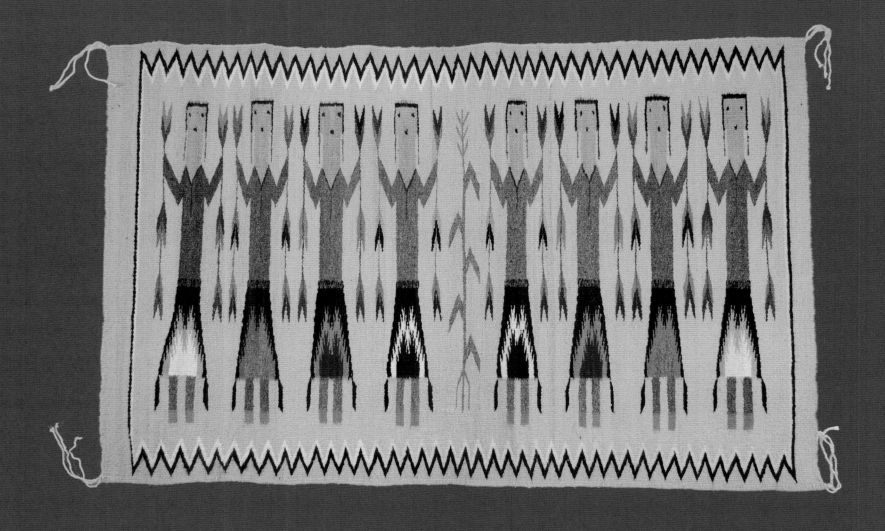

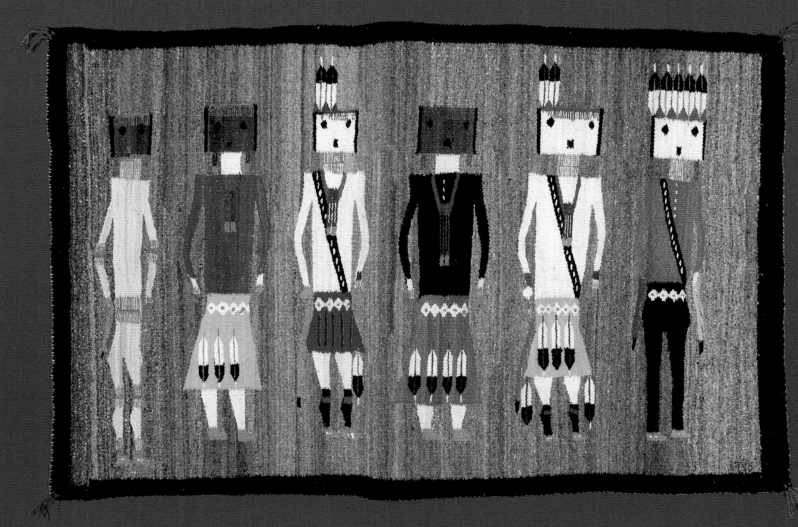

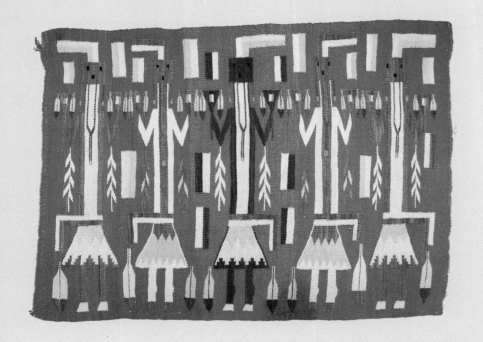

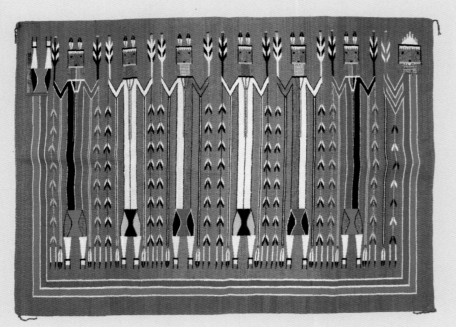

Messengers from the Gods

NAVAJO • ARIZONA AND NEW MEXICO

To the Navajo, the *Yei* are Holy People, spirit messengers between the gods and the tribal community. During healing ceremonies such as the Night Way, also known as the Night Chant, *Yei* are invoked to restore balance and harmony, two important facets of spiritual health in the Navajo worldview. Dancing masked figures known as *Yeibichai* embody the sacred messengers. Ceremonial sand paintings that incorporate *Yei* are created by medicine men during these rituals. Afterward they are promptly destroyed, for they are meant only for Native eyes, and their healing power lies in their ephemerality.

In the early 20th century, Navajo artisans began to include pictorial imagery in their textile designs. Some were controversial replicas of sand paintings, such as the early portrayals of *Yei* and chantway ceremonies woven by the medicine man Hosteen Klah. Today, however, blankets with *Yei* or *Yeibichai* images are not considered sacred, as they intentionally do not recreate an entire sand painting. They exist instead as powerful, striking compositions in their own right, testifying to the importance of healing rituals. Rainbow borders are attributed to the Rainbow God, and may signify the sovereignty of the Navajo nation, *near left middle and bottom.*

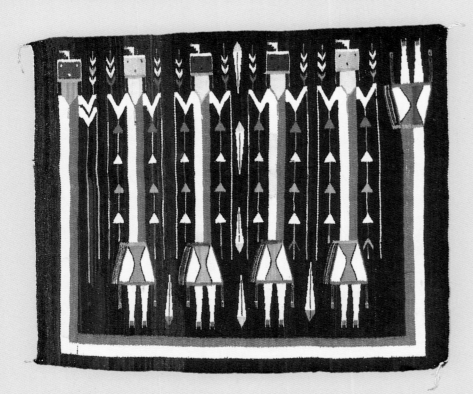

Powerful Figures

Yeibichai blankets are distinguishable by the thicker, more humanlike figures of the dancers, *far left bottom. Yei*, in contrast, have elongated bodies, *left top, far left top.* They almost always appear with images of corn and cornstalks. The geometric shapes that hang from their bent arms are often interpreted as strings of prayer feathers.

Where Earth Meets Sky

Symmetry, balance, and order—these central tenets of American Indian medicine manifest themselves perfectly in the austere geometry of Navajo sand paintings, such as *Mother Earth, Father Sky* by Joe Ben Jr., *left*. The creation of such paintings plays an integral role in the healing process. First, a medicine person carefully layers sand, which is usually dyed in four colors that represent the ultimate balance of the cardinal directions. The patient then sits directly on the sacred painting as the medicine person touches the patient to restore psychic balance and enhance well-being. After the ritual, the sand painting is ceremoniously swept up and buried. The example pictured here, however, was not created for use in a healing ceremony; its fine sand has been secured by a bonding agent.

The pattern pictured here is a common one among sand painters. From the body of Mother Earth rise the four most sacred plants—tobacco, corn, beans, and squash—while Father Earth wears the mantle of the sky, including its constellations and the horned sun and moon. A line of pollen connects the two figures, symbolizing fertility. The rainbow strip that stretches about the perimeter is meant to protect against malevolent forces; it opens toward the east, allowing positive forces to enter and heal the patient's imbalance.

Singing Down the Rain

TOHONO O'ODHAM • ARIZONA

In a parched desert where summer temperatures regularly exceed 120°F, rain is essential to life. Over countless centuries, the Tohono O'odham of southern Arizona have learned to work in harmony with the land to harness its sustaining—yet scarce—resources. *Nawait*, the Rain Ceremony conducted each June to pull down the clouds and bring blessed rain, is a vital part of life for the people. The rites also mark the beginning of a new year.

Saguaro, *right*, features prominently in *Nawait*. In the early morning, the community harvests the thorny fruits from the cactus's high reaches, using dried ribs of old saguaro, *far right*. Back at camp, the fruit is peeled, strained, and condensed into a syrup, which bubbles by a fire for two nights until it ferments. Tohono O'odham men then imbibe the saguaro wine, reciting poems or songs to invoke the rain. In this way, they drink the wine just as the earth drinks the rain.

Saguaro Fruits

Saguaro's summer blooms give way to generously sized fruits, *above*. Today, Tohono O'odham community members are striving to revive the important *Nawait* ceremony, which reinforces the once-fundamental relationship between this land and its people.

The Story of *Nawait*

Long ago, the Desert People's leader accidentally exiled the wind from the tribal homelands. Taking along its friend the frail and fragile rain, the wind departed, and the desert soon dried up. Humans and animals all suffered. Coyote, bear, and vulture used their powers to search for the pair, but to no avail.

Tiny hummingbird volunteered to find the wind and rain, even though others doubted it would be successful. Using its delicate, downy feathers, the hummingbird felt a faint breeze, and followed it to a faraway cave where the wind and rain resided. Rejoicing, the Desert People welcomed the elements home. To this day, the *Nawait* Rain Ceremony celebrates the life-giving qualities of the wind and rain that sustain the people.

Recreating the World

PLAINS TRIBES

As the days lengthen on the North American flatlands, the Plains tribes gather to celebrate one of their most sacred and complex ceremonies, the Sun Dance. This rite marks both the earth's annual regeneration and the people's spiritual renewal. Participants abstain from food and water for up to four days, and dance from morning to night. Before the highly spiritual ceremony, they build a lodge, staking a consecrated tree at the center as the link between sky and earth. This tree is decorated with a bison head or other offerings, and participants dance forwards to and backwards from the tree. In the 1800s, some dancers threaded bone pieces into their skin, tethering themselves to the tree. As they danced, the pieces broke through their flesh, symbolizing their sacrifice and rejuvenation.

Constructing the Sun Dance Lodge

After a ceremony honoring the cottonwood tree, which was chosen as the 2004 Shoshone Sun Dance lodge's sacred center pole, tribal member Jake Hill makes the first cut, *above*. A completed Crow-Shoshone Sun Dance lodge from the 1990s shows the circular, open-frame construction, *left*, typical of most lodges.

Collective Prayers

The highly ritualized Sun Dance, also known as the Medicine Lodge Ceremony, imitates the re-creation of the world. The round lodge with its revered tree, or *axis mundi*, represents this sacred world, and participants who enter into it offer themselves up in thanksgiving for the gift of life. Eagle feathers stand at attention on the heads of observers in a portion of a 19th-century bison hide painting, possibly Sioux in origin, *left*. Bright colors evoke the social and spiritual energy of the ceremony in a 19th-century Shoshone Katsikodi School painting, *above*. A large drum is visible in the lower left-hand corner, as are the singers. Offerings fly high above the sacred tree, which symbolically as well as literally centers the ceremony. Banned by the federal government from the mid-1880s to 1933, the Sun Dance remains a significant part of religious life for many Plains tribes.

Power of the Drum

Sometimes called the heartbeat of the earth, medicinal drums are an important part of the healing process for many tribes. They are often employed in curing ceremonies; without their steady rhythm, many dances—prayers made visible—would be unable to take form. Such drums were created to reflect the power or spirit guardian of their owners or to tell a story important to a tribe, and they could be played individually or as part of a larger drum circle.

"To the Blackfeet, Napi represents the spectrum of what it means to be human. He is both trickster and wise hero, and we are created in his extraordinary image.... My art reflects the beauty of my heritage, which should be shared and passed on to upcoming generations."

Darrell Norman, Blackfeet

Napi and the Gift of Life

This re-creation of a medicine drum, *right*, formed and painted by Blackfeet artist Darrell Norman, is inspired by the symbolism of the Blackfeet creation story and by the ceremony of the Medicine Pipe, or Thunder Pipe Society, or which Norman is a member. According to Blackfeet history, *Napi*—powerful spirit and cultural hero—drew forth the first plants, humans, and all life from the endless sea. Tadpoles struggling to the surface in spring represent the continuity of life. The moon, the sun, and their son, the blue morning star that arcs in the dark sky, keep watch over *Napi* as he shapes mud into man and woman. Imitation eagle feathers strung on a beaded strand attached to the drum remind us of the healing powers of the medicine pipe.

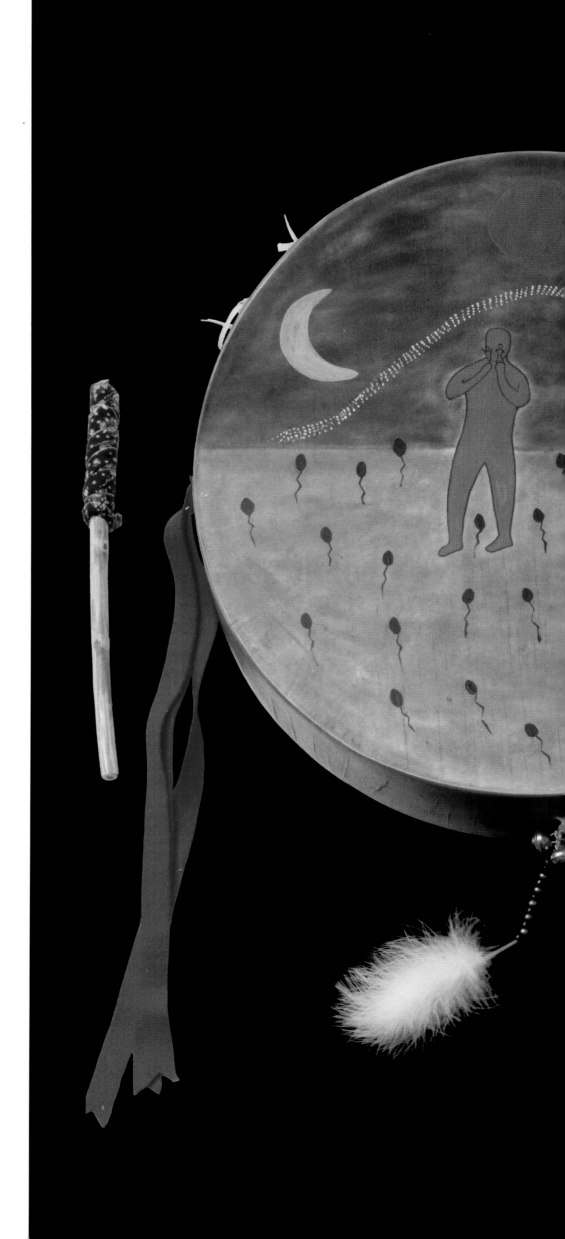

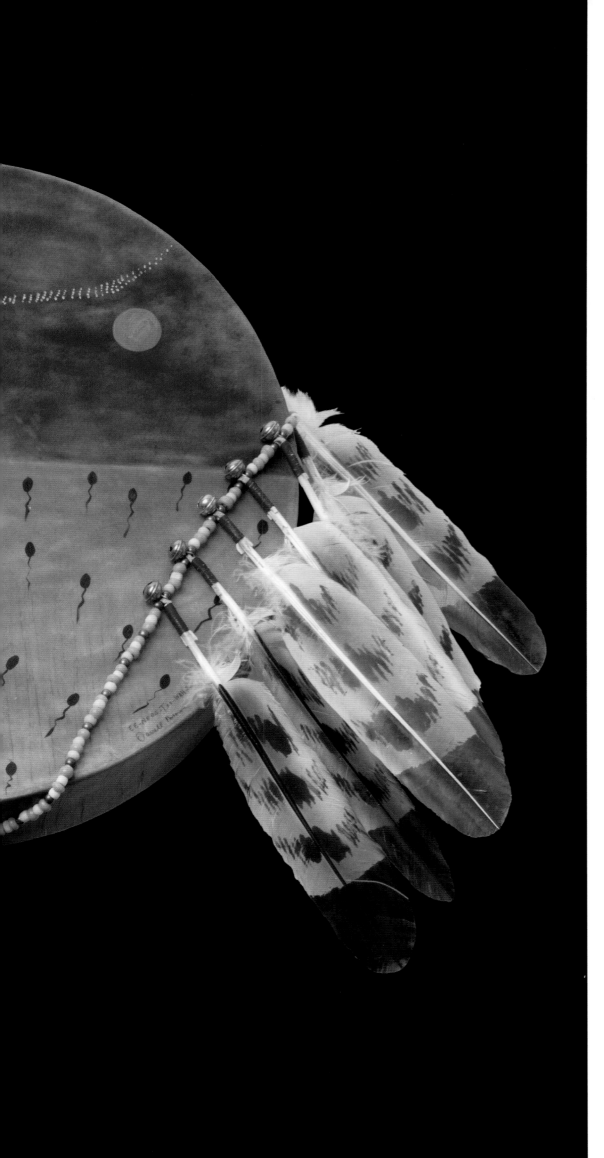

Hunkpapa Lakota Medicine Drum

The striking shape of this hide drum, *above*, marks it as the property of Tatanka Yotanka. Also known as Sitting Bull, this powerful Lakota medicine man and chief is considered to be the last Sioux to surrender to the federal government. Sitting Bull was hailed as a powerful spiritual leader and was an active participant in the sacred Plains Sun Dance. Although he passed away in 1890, the power of this unusual drum still resonates. Most Lakota medicine drums were round, so this example is unique for its square shape, as well as for the two horns that arch gracefully from its top corners. While the buffalo on the drum likely referenced Sitting Bull's name, it may also have channeled the strength of the animal.

Old-growth cypress rise like quiet giants from the bayous of Southern Louisiana; according to the Chitimacha tribe of the region, when the Great Spirit made the world from his own body there was nothing but water, hiding the earth. The present-day scene at Lake Fausse Point State Park, a 6,000-acre wilderness in the Atchafalaya Basin, evidences this. The Chitimacha also believe that a great cypress similar to the trees above

marked one of the four corners of their world. The tribe developed settlements around these bayous, and may have even maintained a ferry system up and down the banks. Though the population suffered under the French and Spanish and early American settlers beginning in the early 1700s, Chitimacha artisans are known today for their intricate single and double-weave baskets, woven from river cane harvested from the bayou.

Ancestral Emblems

Animals walk the earth's round surface, surrounding the mythic female *Maka* in this 1988 painting, *The Pregnant Grandfather* by Oglala Sioux artist Colleen Cutschall, *above*. This spectrum of animals—raccoon to wolf to moose—is telling, as some were used for food or skins, while others occupied a place of spiritual and narrative power. These particular animals came in dreams as messengers of spiritual power, or became the basis for a clan motif. Clan or moiety systems, which organized many tribal societies, were often named after those animals considered to be the first humans' ancestors. A person born into a clan identified with that animal for life. To the Tlingit of Alaska, animals and humans share the same past. Eagle, killer whale, and seal pipe heads, *far right*, were personal items carried by a man for ritual smoking. A pipe's animal was often influenced by what the carver saw in the raw material. The grain of the wood may have looked like the feathered wing of the eagle, *far right top*. The animals on a shaman's oystercatcher rattle, *near right*, were carefully chosen, for they imbued the rattle with symbolic meaning. When shamans used rattles, it was the presence of the animals and the sound the rattles made that helped the shaman cure most sicknesses. In this example, created between 1830 and 1860, a large frog lies beneath a human figure; its twisted hair, grasped in the raven's beak, may indicate that the human is a tortured witch.

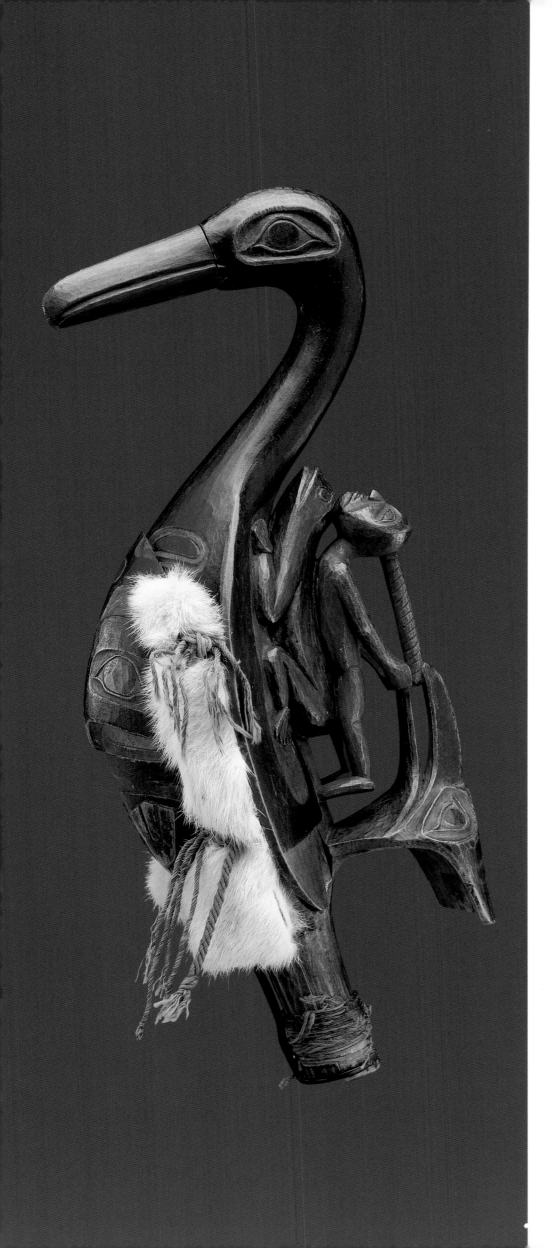

Evoking the Powers of Animals

Due to their proximity to the land, tribes formed intimate relationships with animals, living beings that thrived and suffered according to the earth's changing conditions. Whether the diligence of the ant or the visual acuity of the eagle, each creature's attributes were carefully observed and then used to inform the animals' roles in Native worldviews. For example, many Southwestern tribes deem the coyote a trickster and a hero, for his actions teach humans the repercussions of positive and negative behavior.

Medicine Wheels

PLAINS TRIBES

Quiet and serene, large rock formations known as medicine wheels were built on isolated and difficult-to-reach mountaintops and plateaus throughout western North America. It is thought that the stone arrangements may illustrate a way of counting of time. Loaf-shaped stones were laid out in a wide circle encircling a center smaller stone ring; a series of stone spokes emanating outward mark the time for the summer solstice.

At an elevation of over 9,000 feet, one of the most well-preserved and important medicine wheels lies on Medicine Mountain in Wyoming's Bighorn Range, *right*. Measuring eighty feet in diameter, twenty-eight rows of stones emanate from a center stone pile. The stone spokes may represent the days in a lunar month, although its function remains a mystery. Regardless, its spiritual power is undiminished, and the Bighorn Medicine Wheel is sacred to many Plains tribes.

Rain Clouds, by Mateo Romero, Cochiti Pueblo

We All Come Together

DR. HENRIETTA MANN • CHEYENNE

> "*These ceremonies—from the rhythmic echo of dancing feet pounding the earth to the sounds of feasting from a bustling potlatch—are often the spiritual, social, cultural, and even political glue that preserves Native worldviews.*"

In the beginning, the Great Mysterious All Spirit created the beautiful and miraculous universe. Within this sacred circle of life, the Creator placed the humble, two-legged walkers and all things necessary for their sustenance. The plant people, winged people, and animal people provided food, clothing, and shelter. Humans were to live out their lives on the surface of the earth their mother, a loving spiritual being who would nourish and nurture them.

Today, American Indian communities come together to pay homage to this interrelatedness and to give thanks for the circle of life that sustains. Through communal song, dance, and feasting, they celebrate and affirm traditions and beliefs. These ceremonies—from the rhythmic echo of dancing feet pounding the earth to the sounds of feasting from a bustling potlatch—are often the spiritual, social, cultural, and even political glue that preserves Native worldviews. Repeated reenactments of these important rituals bring the participant back to those elements that make all life possible.

This circle of life remains all-encompassing, for the path human beings walk is long, extending back to creation and forward into an unknown future. They find strength through the land that binds them to one another, and through the gifts of food that the land provides. Indeed, feasts, festivals, and ceremonies continue to revere and honor essential foods and foodways that have nourished Native peoples through the ages. The four main foods that best represent this relationship are water, berries, corn, and meat, and each figures prominently in celebrations and gatherings across Indian Country.

At the beginning of time there was water, which is necessary for all life and has many healing powers. During the Northern Cheyenne Water Prayer, a container of water is prayed over, and those who drink it receive blessings or are healed. Medicine people continue to sing to the water spirits, never taking water's life-giving powers for granted. The liquid also manifests as rain in many ceremonies.

125

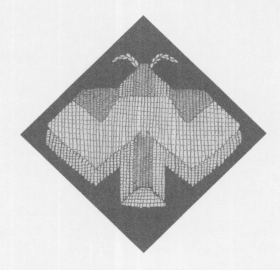

Seen from the flat mesas of New Mexico, approaching clouds tower majestically over the desert landscape. Water imagery is ubiquitous in ceremonies calling forth the rain. Commonly used symbols include frogs, dragonflies, rain clouds, and butterflies, *above top and bottom*.

"To encourage abundance, Tlingit tribal members offered up heaps of precious and nourishing salmon roe (eggs) to the spirits of the berries."

Rain is essential to crop growth, and imagery of rain, clouds and lightning plays a part in many Pueblo agricultural dances. Male dancers softly shake gourd rattles, a sound that mimics gentle summer showers; beautifully embroidered borders on female dance *mantas,* or aprons, symbolize rain and cloud formations.

Water performs a significant role in other Plains Indian ceremonies by its very absence. As an act of personal sacrifice, an individual vows to abstain from drinking water for a specified number of days. Such fasts are common, and participants engage in them individually or collectively. Men performing Plains Indian Sun Dances (more than twenty tribes practice some form of the ceremony) dance in the intensely hot summer sun without benefit of shade, and forgo water and food for an average of four days and nights. This ritual ranks as a great sacrifice and is not lightly undertaken. The entire community provides spiritual support to the man undergoing such a rigorous exercise in self-restraint, singing and drumming to encourage him.

Though water is necessary to all life, many Indians also consider berries to be of divine importance. In fact, one Ojibwe-Chippewa tradition warns that the road to the afterlife is paved not with good intentions, but with delicious, luscious berries that tempt the soul to stop and enjoy instead of continuing on the journey. Tart or sweet, blue, ruby, or violet, the type of berry a tribe revered depended on the environment in which the tribe lived, and often berries were one of the few sources of sugar and sweetness. In Alaska's Glacier Bay, the Tlingit people once harvested more than nineteen varieties of berry—including the cloudberry, bearberry, and thimbleberry. Berries also played a vital role in trade: exchanged as currency, gifted to notable tribal members, or transformed into soap and other goods, they helped forge and maintain connections among tribes. So important were some patches of berry bushes to the Tlingit that tribal members named them and tended them in the hope that they would thrive. To encourage abundance, Tlingit tribal members offered up heaps of precious and nourishing salmon roe (eggs) to the spirits of the berries. From the Iroquois Strawberry Festival to the huckleberry feasts of the Yakama and Warm Springs tribes of Oregon, berries are still the focus of seasonal reverence and a key ingredient in both secular and ceremonial dishes. For example, the Lakota Sioux build on the tradition of their mothers by making *wojape* pudding from the flavorful chokecherry, boiling down a pot of the pitted berries, adding honey if available, and enjoying the dish as a summertime delicacy.

The late San Ildefonso artist J. D. Roybal brings a Pueblo feast day to life in his work *Corn Dancers, above*. A striped *koshare* figure leads a procession of alternating male and female dancers, while the *kiva* in the background bustles with ritual activity.

Farther south, along the banks of the sweet Rio Grande and atop New Mexico's mesas, the nineteen Pueblos celebrate the vital qualities of the spirits of animals, the Three Sisters, and other foods. Syncretic daylong feasts achieve a balance between the two religions, simultaneously honoring a tribe's Catholic patron saint and—through Native dances—elk, buffalo, deer, or corn. Corn Dances are a focal point, as corn was once the staple crop of the Pueblo people. Corn Mother or Corn Woman, as the food is personified, represents life, growth, and femininity, and tribes perform corn dances as entreaties for rain, abundance of crops, fertility, and the tribe's general well-being. Dancers may carry ears of mature corn, for they symbolize the rich fullness of fertilization. Feast days, which may occur once or several times annually, present a chance for communities to gather and celebrate with family and friends. Tribal members rise with the sun to celebrate Mass, and then move in procession to the central plaza for a daylong series of

A Mandan man stands attired in buffalo dance regalia in a circa 1908 photo, *above*.

traditional dances. Multiple generations of the community dance together in long lines in most of these, accompanied by song and the resonant drum. At the very end of the moving line, the very youngest learn the steps by following their elders.

Plains Indians knew well the buffalo's importance in sustaining life, as the animal provided skins for homes and clothing, bones and horn for tools, rawhide for parfleche, and organs for cooking pots. Most important, it supplied food. The average buffalo weighed more than 1,600 pounds, and a successful hunt provided ample quantities of meat and fat, which could be dried and stored for later use. Feasts often preceded or followed such hunts, thanking the buffalo for its sacrifice through song, dance, and ritual. Each year, the Mandan tribe of the Upper Missouri River celebrated the buffalo during the four-day Okipa ceremony before a buffalo hunt. During their buffalo dance, Okipa dancers impersonated the animal, wearing tanned buffalo hides, horns, and buffalo hair around their wrists and ankles. Such dancing lured the buffalo close to the village and helped ensure a successful hunt.

Some feasts incorporate all of the four sacred foods. After an all-night prayer meeting of the Native American Church of North America (NAC)—a pan-Indian religion that uses peyote buttons taken from the cactus plant as a divine medicine—participants consume a feast of water, berries, corn, and meat. Prior to this communal feast, a woman brings in the morning water. Sitting on the ground before a consecrated fire, she prays over the water for all life on earth. Those partaking in the ceremony then pass around the water, and later all enjoy a festive meal, a medley of the four ingredients so important to all tribes.

Contemporary Native America continues to honor its traditional foods, some of which Indians still gather and harvest as they did in the beginning. Feasts and festivals abound that tell the stories of these plants, animals, and creatures of the air, land, and sea. The simple offering of a cornmeal prayer to the wind is as meaningful, and as powerful, as any elaborate harvest thanksgiving feast. Through feast and festival, food is both medium and celebrant, always the honored guest.

Corn stalks and lightning bolts pierce through white clouds in the Hopi artist Dawakema Milland Lomakema's *Corn People of the Four Directions*, *right*.

Pueblo *Tablitas*

Stairstep patterning mirrors the strata of rain clouds on the carved wooden *tablitas* worn by Pueblo women during the Corn Dance, which is sometimes called the *Tablita* Dance. Stylized red, yellow, and blue cornstalks adorn a *tablita* created circa 1890–1910, *right*, while butterflies spread their wings on more recent Santa Clara examples, *above and far right*. Sacred eagle down feathers atop the *tablitas* move as the women shift from foot to foot.

A Dance Before Planting

PUEBLO TRIBES • NEW MEXICO

Moving in unison, moccasin-clad feet softly tamp the earth of a pueblo's center plaza. It is spring, and Pueblo men and women have come together to pray for rain, which will in turn bring forth life-sustaining corn. This public dance was traditionally held before planting, and dancers would come adorned with symbols and colors of the earth's fertility: blue and white clouds, rain and lightning, and yellow and blue-gray corn. As they move in two parallel lines, the men shake gourd rattles and carry verdant bunches of evergreen boughs, while the women wear colorfully painted wooden *tablitas*.

Taken together, the symbols, the drum and its singers, and the mental and physical intentions of the dancers comprise a communal invocation that honors the cycle of the seasons and unites Father Sky with Mother Earth. The Corn Dance may fall on a pueblo's Feast Day, which honors that tribe's patron saint while incorporating elements of the Native worldview, such as this prayer made visible.

History of the Potlatch

TRIBES OF ALASKA AND THE PACIFIC NORTHWEST

During long winter months when the sun only briefly lit the frozen earth, Northwestern and Alaskan tribes held ceremonial gatherings. Of these, the potlatch—from Chinook trade jargon meaning "to give"—was paramount in reinforcing political and economic relationships among family groups and villages. Potlatches also honored the dead and enabled the potlatch host to rise in rank through elaborate displays and gifts of tangible wealth. Status depended on the riches one could bestow on others—not amass for oneself. A host might give away blankets, animal skins, dishes, baskets, beads, or even slaves throughout the multiday ceremony. Turn-of-the-20th-century Tlingit men, dressed in distinguished finery before entering a longhouse for a potlatch, *above*, enjoyed song, dance, formal recitations of history, and, of course, a glorious feast.

Spruce Root Potlatch Hat

Four "nobility" or "potlatch" rings rise proudly from this circa 1840 Tlingit potlatch hat, *right*. The rings represent the number of potlatches given by its owner, a high-ranking Raven clan leader from Sitka, Alaska. A silky, white ermine pelt cascades onto the brim, whose designs may represent killer whale, raven, salmon, or Mouse Woman.

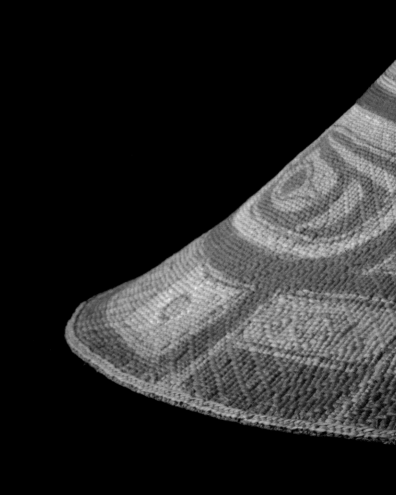

Paddle to Lummi

LUMMI • WASHINGTON

On July 30, 2007, the swift strokes of canoe paddles stirred the normally still waters of Bellingham Bay, as the Lummi Nation joyously welcomed seventy-three canoes to its banks. Forty-five tribes, coming from as far away as Juneau, Alaska, made the ceremonial trip along the coast to inaugurate Lummi's first potlatch in more than seventy years. Northwest tribes alternately volunteer to host this event, which is the twelfth of its kind since the practice was revived in 1989. Tribes who undertake the enormous commitment to host a potlatch are honored for their reinvigoration of tribal customs, and for their efforts to inspire youth to carry on traditions in danger of being lost.

Lummi elders believe that canoe journeys help the tribe and its people achieve harmony and balance. Such journeys also pay homage to the historic use of the Northwest coast's many waterways for transportation, food, trade, and festivity—which is a centuries-old tradition among Coastal Salish people.

Traveling the Traditional Highways

Canoers arrive on Lummi shores with smiles and raised paddles, which signify to those on shore that they come in peace, *left bottom, right top and bottom*. Awaiting them, tribal members wearing traditional regalia drum a welcome song for their guests, *left top*. Over eight days, the Lummi Nation hosted more than 65,000 visitors, and—in the spirit of the potlatch—distributed thousands of gifts.

"In the re-creation of our history, it takes the mind, spirit, and soul to live and breathe an experience. The Muckleshoot potlatch gave everyone in our community an opportunity to live, breathe, and experience a potlatch that was conducted in the way of our ancestors."

Walter Pacheco, Captain of the Muckleshoot Canoe Family

Gathering Together

MUCKLESHOOT • WASHINGTON

Retracing their ancestral thoroughfares, more than sixty canoes arrived at Muckleshoot in 2006 to begin the potlatch celebration. Ten months of intense preparations were needed to feed, shelter, and entertain the tens of thousands of visitors. Tribal members crafted thousands of gifts for the potlatch guests, and then a small army of exuberant Muckleshoot children handed out the bounty. Significant gifts included one hundred hand-painted drums donated by students from the tribal college, carved paddles, and Pendleton blankets. The blankets are the greatest honor bestowed in formal situations among Pacific Northwest Coast tribes.

Gifts of Song and Dance

On a sunny day, the active dome of Mount Rainier gleams with white snow, *left*. The volcano is sacred to the Muckleshoot, and provides a fitting backdrop for such a momentous occasion. Tribal volunteers created ceremonial regalia to wear and resurrected important historic songs and dances to share with their guests. Some canoe families in turn bestowed on the Muckleshoot the honor of letting them sing treasured family songs, *above*, which are privately owned like property and gifted on special occasions. A ninety-foot-long dance floor, created especially for the event, was considered sacred space, since it was there that the songs and dances came to life.

A Ceremony of World Renewal

To tribes of the Northeast and Southeast, the Green Corn Dance celebrates and honors the abundance of corn. The ceremony, called *Busk* by some tribes, also marks the new year and is a time for purification of the earth. During the multiday ceremony, most of which takes place on a special square ground, a priest lights a sacred fire composed of logs that point in the four cardinal directions. Appointed clan members gather around the fire, sitting in arbors of latticed branches, as in the colorful painting by Oklahoma Seminole artist Fred Beaver, *left*. The ceremony is an expression of community and thankfulness, witnessed in this recent Seminole Green Corn Dance, *above*.

Testament to Abundance

Most American Indian festivals, whether religious or secular, involve some form of feasting. Serving dishes were specially crafted for use on these special occasions; graceful lines, careful artistry, and extra flourishes characterize bowls, food boxes, and ladles. Some dishes were created for a specific festival; for example, the Wasco-Wishxam of the Columbia River carved exquisite bowls from the horns of bighorn sheep for their annual root-gathering festivals. Faces carved into the underside of this horn bowl, created between 1800 and 1850, *near left bottom*, may represent the earth's guardian spirits, who are honored during the feast. Freshly gathered roots were placed in the bowl as part of a ritual meal.

Feast Dishes

Spectacular Haida ceremonial dishes were passed hand-to-hand during potlatch feasts. A deeply curved bowl shaped like a proud seal, *near left top*, held seal or eulachon oil, while two bent-corner dishes held berries, salmon, or other delectables. The yew wood dish, *near left middle*, circa 1780, is remarkable for its age and for its bulging sides, which may be seen as a metaphor for the bounty of its creator. A thinner, more delicate dish, *far left bottom*, is decorated with thirty-two opercula of the rare red turban snail.

Male and female spirit effigies observe each other across the wide expanse of a two-hundred-year-old feast bowl, *far left top*. This Northeastern Woodlands dish is delicately rimmed in black pigment, binding the male (who wears a warrior's roached hairstyle) on the right with the female on the left.

Hopi Eagle Dance, by Dan Namingha, Tewa/Hopi

Songs to the Spirits

IRIS HEAVYRUNNER-PRETTY PAINT • BLACKFEET/CROW

"Today, the Hoop Dance reminds us of the harmony between tradition and innovation made possible when the foundation of cultural patterning is recognized and embraced."

Hoops dazzle as a dancer navigates the intricate steps of the Hoop Dance, a spectacular performance piece. Over years of training, a Hoop Dancer learns to manipulate more than forty hoops around his body to form the shapes of butterflies, eagles, turtles, or the roundness of the earth; the dance is a blur of quick footwork and precise movement. Hoops, which symbolize the endless cycles contained within the larger circle of life, were once used ceremonially by healers, but today's Hoop Dancers execute the steps only for entertainment. Regardless, layered within the dancer's postures and movements are important patterns of deeply rooted American Indian traditions. A Hoop Dancer must learn and perfect the complicated hoop work, anticipate the song's rhythm, and balance creativity with accuracy, showmanship, and speed. Today, the Hoop Dance reminds us of the harmony between tradition and innovation made possible when the foundation of cultural patterning is recognized and embraced.

Repeated patterns of music and movement recall the feelings and memories of a people. Patterns are evident in all things: the lacing of a rawhide drum, the carved strokes of a dance mask, a rattle's rippled turtle shell, and the warp and weft of a woven basket. Like these tangible objects, tribal songs and dances also have patterns; singers create them through rhythm and melody, dancers through gesture. Though these patterns vary according to geographic area, tribe, ceremony, or even family, they are recognizable to a casual observer. This is because the intention behind the formation of those patterns—whether social, celebratory, or prayerful—is ubiquitous across tribal boundaries. Patterns are also found in how songs and dances are inherited—music passed down to respected song keepers and drummers, and dances learned through carefully tracing the steps of the elders. Cultural patterns help one remember the songs and dances, which were historically not recorded, yet are interwoven in everything we stand for. There are patterns in our daily lives, and in our prayers.

Led by Bill Baker, the famed Mandaree Singers, *right*, traveled throughout Indian Country singing at powwows and honor ceremonies. This photo, taken at a South Dakota powwow in 1992, shows members of the group preparing to sing.

"*Understanding the songs takes more than memorizing words or melodies—it involves deep observation of community and ritual, listening and sharing stories and songs, and serving the needs of the people. It is, in essence, committing the patterns of a people to heart.*"

Without knowing a particular song, a knowledgeable listener can usually discern the tribal or regional origin of a song from the vocal style, instrumentation, rhythm, and direction of the melody. The Mandaree Singers of North Dakota, for example, are known for their distinct harmony, which sounds like one voice singing, and for the rapid beat of their drumming. These patterns testify to the importance of music and movement to strengthen the oral legacy of Native people.

Seasoned dancers are closely attuned to the subtle shifts in beat or tone made by the drum and singers. Awareness of the song, honed over years of practice, is as important as any other learned tradition. In our music, whether sacred or secular, the voice is considered the most important instrument, and in some tribes, song keepers are chosen to keep these heirloom treasures alive for the people and for future generations. John G. Myers is one of these, a gifted song keeper from the Chippewa Cree Nation. He entered the Sun Dance circle at the age of five when his mother asked him to carry a medicine bundle on his back from the Haystack community to the dance arbor. At that young age, he came to understand that he was carrying the prayers for his people—a great responsibility—and he was chosen by his grandfather, John Good Runner, to be the song keeper.

Within Montana tribal communities—especially among the elders—song keepers are highly respected, and are often deeply religious. Not only do they memorize long songs and the stories behind them, but they teach their uniquely nuanced songs to younger generations, acting as interpreters. All who assume the mantle of song keeper follow a pattern of involved learning. Understanding the songs

takes more than memorizing words or melodies—it involves deep observation of community and ritual, listening and sharing stories and songs, and serving the needs of the people. It is, in essence, committing the patterns of a people to heart.

Without these patterns, song and dance lose their meaning. Context is critical because our songs and dances are understood only in relation to other Native traditions: language, customs, seasons, or life cycle events. Rituals of music and movement bestow power and purpose and reinforce personal and communal relationships. Not only are the songs rich with history, they also reflect the natural changes and complexities of a living culture. Meaningful relationships support our vision of success and allow creativity to flourish.

American Indian music does not rely on words alone to convey a song's meaning. Instruments—from percussion to the more unusual stringed varieties—create varying tempos and tones depending on the nature of the song. Drums may be played either by an individual, or by a group using many drumsticks on a rawhide surface. Whistles and flutes, often decorated with symbolic animal motifs, create evocative, haunting tones. Dancers often carry rattles: used by most tribes and thought of as highly sacred, rattles are crafted from hollowed gourds, shell, or hooves, and are employed to great effect.

Overlaying these rhythms are the songs themselves, composed or remembered by lead singers. Interestingly, many songs are composed primarily of vocables, which are syllables that have no linguistic meaning. Vocables are crucial to the transference of songs over generations and across tribes and regions, for they

A Cheyenne whistle, *above,* and a Laguna rattle, *bottom,* were used in dances, or were played alone. The Laguna rattle was tied to a dancer's leg and jingled with each step.

A young Choctaw/Chickasaw boy shows promise as he manipulates his hoops, *above*, at a 2002 powwow in Natchez, Mississippi.

"*Dancing gives ancestral traditions new life, responding to family and community needs. With each generation, a dance finds ways to create new patterns.*"

Used in the Grass Dance, this Pawnee double-sided drum, *right*, vividly depicts the ritual. Swallows in a yellow sky herald Thunderbird's arrival as he dives through heavy clouds that shield two red birds issuing lightning from their eyes. The Pawnee call thunder "the hissing of the great snake," and the Grass Dance holds the Thunderbird as its protector.

eliminate the need for a common language. These syllables may sound unintelligible to the untrained ear, but vocable composition actually follows a strict format. Since most traditional Grass Dances and honor songs are quite long, slight shifts in vocables alert dancers to the song's approaching end, ensuring that no one moves beyond the final beat of the music.

American Indians dance for many reasons. Ceremonial dances, which are usually not performed for non-Natives, can be long, complex affairs. Social dances are often shortened permutations of ceremonial dances: with sacred elements removed, they are appropriate to share. The Hoop Dance, performed by many Plains Nations, is one example. Within a tribe, the act of dancing is multilayered. Johnny Arlee, a Salish cultural ambassador, believes that dancing helps Salish youths take pride in who they are. Dancing gives ancestral traditions new life, responding to family and community needs. With each generation, a dance finds ways to create new patterns.

Though we differ in our histories, worldviews, languages, and customs, as tribal people we share a desire to preserve and promote our way of life. We do this through the rhythms of our drums, rattles, flutes, and whistles, and through the movements we make in the accompanying dance. Through the instruments' voices and our own motions of veneration, our culture's power is made both visible and audible, claiming its place in the universe. Ceremonial and social song and dance are more than notes sung or steps taken; they are the wisdom of our people, expressed through music and movement.

Invoking the *Gaan*

WHITE MOUNTAIN APACHE • ARIZONA

Crown Dancers are the embodiment of *Gaan*, or the Apache Mountain spirits, and are a physical manifestation of the spirit world. They traditionally dance to protect the people by banishing evil, epidemics, and enemies. Appearing during Apache Sunrise Ceremonies, the dancers enter from the east, like the sun, and move to the beat of the singer's water drum.

"We need to keep our traditions alive. We need to pass on our traditional and cultural ways to the children."

Joe Tohonnie Jr., White Mountain
Apache/Navajo

Crown Dancers

Crown Dancers are so named for their painted wooden-slat headpieces, which are used to great effect to imitate the quick movements of the butterfly and hummingbird. In Western Apache Crown Dancing, a bull-roarer, which is twirled on a length of rope and produces a resonating wind-sound, accompanies the drumming and singing of the *Gaan* songs. This young group of White Mountain Apache Crown Dancers, *near and far left*, represents five different Apache bands. The band travels throughout Indian Country, performing with celebrated singer Joe Tohonnie Jr., *above*.

The Stomp Dance

CREEK • GEORGIA

The highly social Stomp Dance appears in the traditions of nearly all East Coast tribes, from Seneca to Seminole. The Creek, however, are its main practitioners today. Associated primarily with the summer Green Corn Festival, Stomp Dances are an integral part of Creek social and ceremonial circles. Representing a time of renewal, the festival requires fasting and several days of sleep deprivation. In fact, the Stomp Dance originated as a way to help Green Corn Festival participants stay awake during times of fasting and prayer.

Male and female participants alternate in the Stomp Dance line, forming a long spiral in a counter-clockwise direction. The steps are also characterized by the constant movements of the body and hands throughout the lengthy days and nights of dancing. Such gesturing weaves the prayers into the smoke of the living fire, which then ascends to the Creator.

Keeping Time

Female Stomp Dancers wear shakers, a type of rattle, on their legs to maintain a rhythm as they dance, *right top*. Historically, shakers were created from terrapin or box turtle shells, *left bottom*, and deer toes—early accounts recall women wearing as many as 1,500 deer toes on one leg. When the Creek were forced to relocate during the Trail of Tears, traditional shaker materials became increasingly scarce. Today, condensed milk cans, *left top and right bottom*, are used because they are lighter, easier to replace, and friendlier to the environment than turtle shells or deer toes. The traditional shakers can still be seen in the more important ceremonies and gatherings, and represent long-standing ties to Creek tradition.

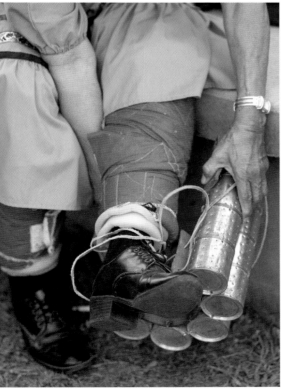

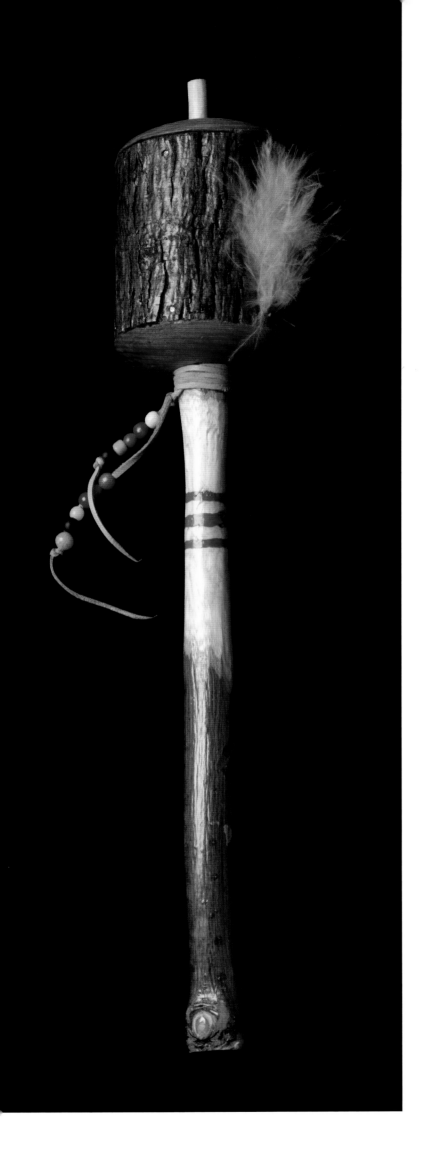

Crafted for Music

Through dance, a culture manifests its worldview; through music, it finds its rhythm. For centuries, American Indian musical instruments—rattles, drums, flutes, whistles, and even fiddles—have accompanied sacred and social ceremonies. They set a beat, mark changes in tempo, and emphasize certain phrases or words important to the song or story being told. The rhythms created by these instruments are both prayer and celebration. Their sounds invoke the strengths and beliefs of the people whose movements complement the expressive tones, as in this San Ildefonso Pueblo Buffalo Dance using drums and rattles, *above.*

A Trio of Rattles

The most common musical instrument among tribes is the rattle. Its soothing sound calls the rain, cures the sick, and accompanies the drum's beat. These contemporary examples show the wide range of styles. The large Jemez gourd rattle by F. Shendo, *far left*, and the for-sale clay rattle by Acoma artist Emma Lewis Mitchell, *left middle*, are adorned with geometric bird motifs. The Seneca Iroquois rattle by Gladys and DeForest Adams, *near left*, is carved from hickory and decorated with leather and beads.

Fiddle to Flute

Dazzling arrays of color, form, and raw material are hallmarks of American Indian musical instruments; these percussive, string, and wind instruments are no exception. An unusual Apache fiddle, *left*, was carved from the stalk of an agave plant, strung with gut, and played for entertainment.

The high-pitched trill of whistles was interpreted differently by various cultures. To the Yup'ik, for example, whistles imitated the high sounds of spirit voices, while to others the tone mimicked a bird. Two views of a clay Zuni whistle, *above*, highlight the sweet curves of an unidentified bird. Masses of dangling feathers and colorful quillwork adorn this Cheyenne dance whistle carved from bone, *near right*, while a simple wooden Sioux flute may have been used in courting, *far right*.

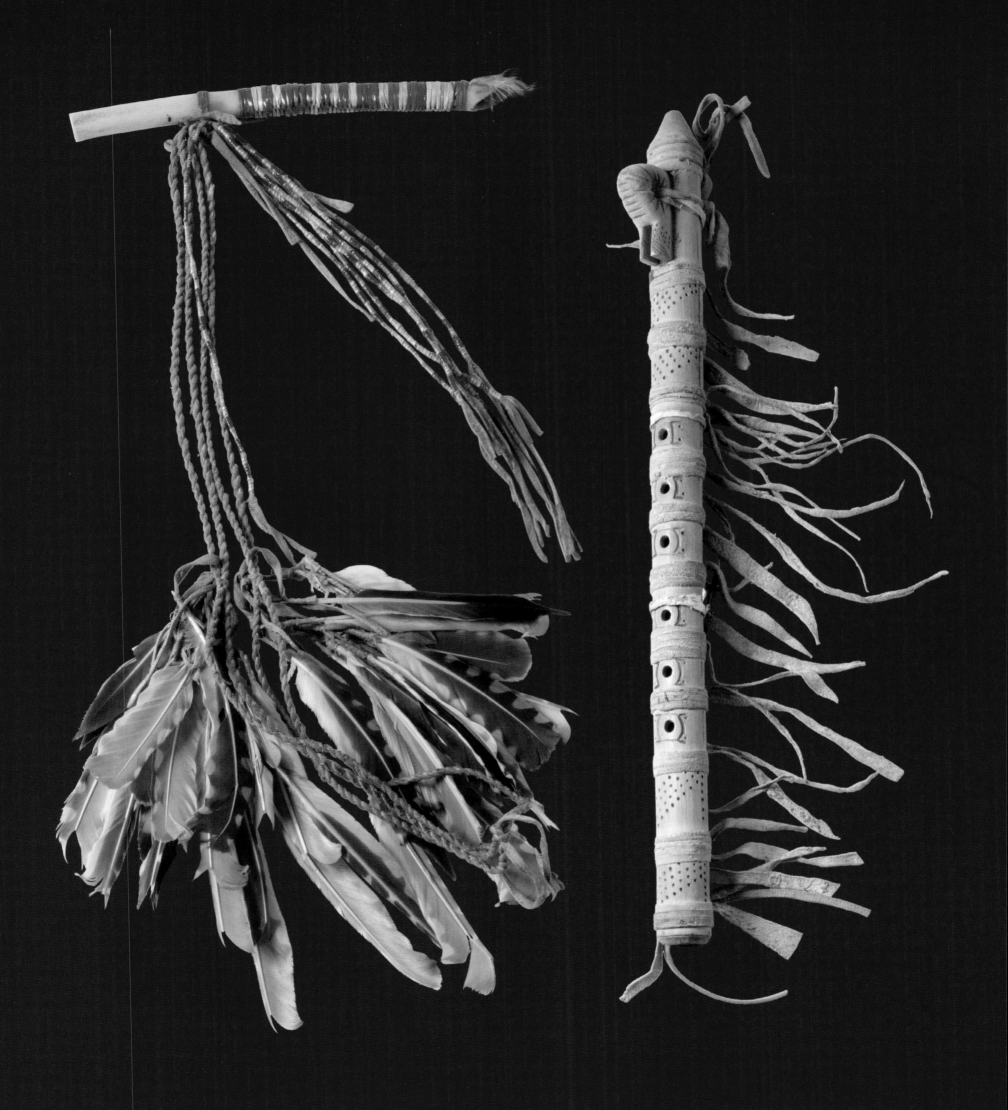

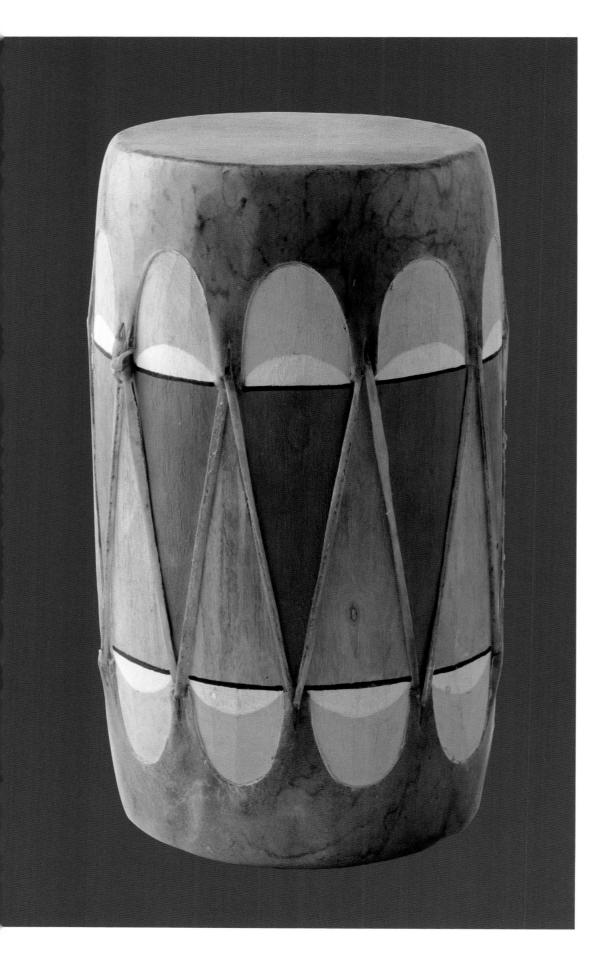

Dance Drums

PUEBLO TRIBES • NEW MEXICO

Crafting a drum calls forth its spirit. Each drum's sound is unique, depending on the type of wood, the thickness of its hide and walls, and the humidity and temperature of its environment. Painted drums with hand-scalloped rawhide tops from Cochiti and Zuni Pueblos, *left and below*, are typical of ceremonial drums.

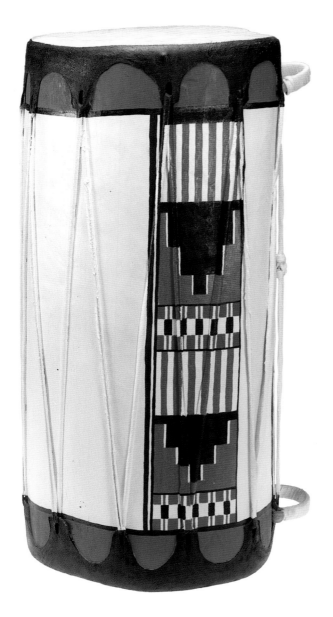

COCHITI INDIAN PUEBLO DRUM MAKERS, NEW MEXICO

A Family Affair

For Pueblo tribes, the carved logs that provided the drum's body were living entities. Therefore, a hole was cut into each carved drum's side to allow it to breathe. Knowledge of the craft, an honored profession, is still passed down through the generations. At Cochiti Pueblo, south of Santa Fe, large water towers painted like drums loom over the high-desert landscape, testifying to the importance of drums and drum making in the community. The Pueblo is esteemed for the fine tone and beauty of its ceremonial drums, which are handcrafted for use by other Pueblo tribes in ceremonial dances, and sold to non-Natives as art objects. This undated photo of a young Cochiti family, *above*, shows a wonderful pile of drums in various stages of their creation, from carved log to completed drum. These would have been made for sale only. The sheer number of drums shows the importance of the craft economically, ceremonially, and symbolically.

Eagle Dancers

Three crouching Eagle Dancers prepare for flight, their wings raised to catch the wind, *left*. Laguna Pueblo, nestled at the base of Mount Taylor, forty-five miles west of Albuquerque, New Mexico, is known for its Eagle Dances. This photo of practicing dancers, taken by honored Laguna Pueblo tribal member and photographer Lee Marmon in 1962, captures both the sacred nature of the dance and the graceful movements of the dancers who imitate the eagle's soaring freedom, tethered only by their long shadows. In turn, the lightness of the eagle represents prayers sent from the people to the gods above. This powerful cosmological symbol is affirmed through the physical impersonation of the men and boys who don the special regalia.

A Place to Dance

PLAINS TRIBES

Though the Grass Dance enjoys a prominent place in contemporary powwow culture, its origins were inspired by a quandary. The dance began in Canada as a way for roaming tribes to work together tamping down the high grasses of the rolling plains—to make room for their tipis, or for dancing. To some tribes like the Cree and Hidatsa, the Grass Dance is a religious ritual never performed for the public.

Today, a modified contemporary-style Grass Dance is popular on the powwow circuit. It offers male participants the opportunity to express and interpret the movements of their landscape, crouching low and swinging one leg out to flatten invisible blades of grass. Grass Dance songs are passed down orally from singer to singer, and follow a relatively strict format of a lead phrase that is repeated and developed over several verses. An ending phrase, often *he-e ye-e- yo*, signifies that the song is nearly over, and dancers, listening carefully, are able to stop on the right musical beat.

Change Over Time

Fringed yarn, ribbons, and streamers mimic the swaying movements of Great Plains grasses as dancers move at a powwow, *left top*. More than one hundred years earlier, Big Foot and his Lakota band stand in simpler—though no less beautiful—Grass Dance regalia, *left bottom*. Plains tribesmen engaged in the dance are frozen in mid-step in this circa 1800 Fereol Bonnemaison ink drawing, *right*.

"My dad always said, if you can sing, share it. Share it, because it is a gift. Do not be afraid."

Sidrick Baker, son of Bill Baker

The Mandaree Singers

MANDAN, HIDATSA, ARIKARA • NORTH DAKOTA

To say the name Bill Baker in powwow circles is to evoke the mastery of one of the most accomplished singers in Indian Country. As the founder of The Mandaree Singers, Baker and his singing group—which included many family members—traveled around the world, singing the Grass Dance and other songs. Instructed by his father and grandfather, Baker soon mastered more than 400 songs and began to compose his own. His group was often selected to be "host drum" at intertribal gatherings, a great honor.

The name "Mandaree" is a combination of Mandan, Hidatsa, and Arikara tribal names, for the three affiliated tribes have comprised the group for more than fifty years. To be allowed to sit and sing showed that a member earned the right to voice the intricate songs—some old, some new—that Baker introduced. Though he passed away in 1993, Baker, *below, near, and far left*, left a legacy of pride in tradition. Today his sons carry on his heritage of sitting around the large drum and sharing their gifts of music with the next generation.

The Paiute people call the Grand Canyon's plateau *Kaibab*, which translates to "Mountain Lying Down." To many tribes, including the Hopi and the Hualapai, the stark beauty of the canyon marks the holy place where their ancestors emerged, and dances are performed at the earth's edge where red rock plunges into the deep gorge below. Landscapes like this one play an integral role in the lives of tribes,

and are recreated and honored through song and dance. Hidatsa and Cree tribes still celebrate their relationship with the Plains through the Grass Dance, while Creek, Seminole, and surviving eastern tribes renew this vital affinity through the Stomp Dance of the Green Corn Festival. Zuni Olla Maidens celebrate their ties to the land by dancing with coiled clay pots, made from earth like that on which they stand.

People of the Salmon

TSIMSHIAN • ALASKA

Guided by the cultural legacy of the Tsimshian of Alaska, and the new compositions of David Boxley, artist and singer, the Git Hoan Dancers are renowned for their powerful presence on stage. Drawing from Tsimshian as well as Tlingit and Haida tribes, the dance troupe travels the world in order to preserve, celebrate, and reinvigorate the song and dance of Tsimshian culture, which ranges up British Columbia's coast to southeastern Alaska.

Though the group now lives near Seattle, most members trace their ancestry to the Tsimshian island village of Metlakatla. The name *Git Hoan* is Tsimshian for "People of the Salmon," for the tribe was—and remains—a seafaring culture.

Today, Git Hoan members perform a variety of dances that honor their heritage, beginning with a song thanking the crowd for inviting them to dance. As the dances continue, the thrum of the cedar box drum keeps a steady rhythm, joyously bringing the stories of a proud people to life.

Git Hoan Dancers

Tristen James calls forth the eagle as she flies across the stage, *near left*. Eagle is identified by his deeply curved beak, which repeats symbolically across her button robe, as well as by the eagle feather fan she carries. Git Hoan dancers, nearly disguised by their raven masks, help tie each other's strings, *far left bottom*. Members of the troupe all dance, sing, and drum as they are needed, *far left top*. The symbolism that adorns their regalia draws directly from the abundant coasts and waters that are home to the Tsimshian, Tlingit, and Haida people. For the Tsimshian, its four clans—eagle, raven, wolf, and killer whale—feature prominently in the strong designs of the Git Hoan ornamentation; in fact, button robes identify the clan to which a dancer belongs.

Masks That Transform

David Robert Boxley, *above*, becomes Mosquito, heeding the wise words of gentle Mouse Woman, *middle top*, in order to live a long and prosperous life. Raven, *far right*, proudly raises his beak, which chatters open and closed at pivotal moments in the song. David Boxley, master carver, brings to life these cultural and mythical heroes from cedar or alder wood. Other masks lie waiting for their turn on stage, such as this brightly painted sleeper mask, *middle bottom*, whose eyes open and shut. The figurative power of these masks—and the dances that enliven them—cannot be overlooked, for with each dance, the Git Hoan troupe reclaims Tsimshian traditions that were nearly lost.

"Songs were property and had value the way a blanket or a canoe had value. They carried weight with them."

David Boxley, Tsimshian

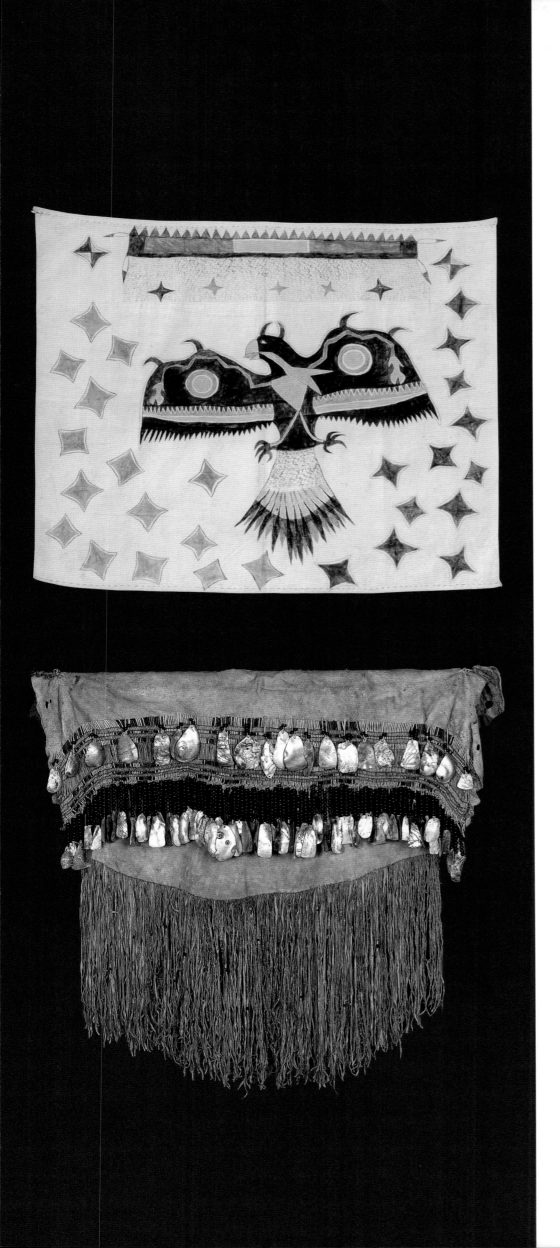

Dance Regalia

Just as dancing affirms the American Indian worldview, so does ceremonial regalia demonstrate the dancer's journey from the time and space of the secular to the sacred. Though materials have evolved over the centuries, the donning of dance clothing—aprons and skirts, masks and fans—is still imperative to the transformative process, whether in ceremony or entertainment. Accessories such as animal pelts, bustles, headpieces, and other symbolic accents contribute to a transcendent aesthetic. While some pieces were made to be worn over and over, some accoutrements, such as masks, were intended only for one ceremonial use.

Aprons and Kilts

Dance clothing was another canvas on which to emphasize the important symbolic elements of a dance. A Hopi cotton and wool dance *manta*, *far left bottom*, was embroidered with alternating butterfly and rain cloud symbols, while the *avanyu*, or water serpent, undulates across the hide of a Tesuque Pueblo dance kilt, *far left top*. The metal cones around the lower border are made from brass rifle cartridges and rolled tin can pieces. For the Hupa of California, dance skirts were heirloom pieces, highly prized by the women who owned them. This deer hide dance skirt, *near left bottom*, is decorated with cobalt-blue trade beads and shimmering abalone shell; for modesty, an apron was worn beneath the skirt. Little is known about this circa 1909 Cheyenne muslin dance apron, *near left top*. One may imagine, however, the effect that the fierce and powerful bird image would have had on the dancing participant.

A New Awareness

To wear a Yup'ik mask is to transform oneself into an animal, or a spirit, or a prayer. Ethereal dance masks—delicate, yet startlingly powerful—are the means through which the Yup'ik worldview is dramatized and understood. Often carved in complementary pairs, they most commonly feature a circle-and-dot motif, through which the universe is personified, or "seen." Wearing them helped channel one's spiritual energy. A contemporary *Man in the Moon* mask by Yup'ik carver John Oscar, *above*, is a striking adaptation of traditional form. The flowing caribou hairs on a Yup'ik woman's dance or "finger" fans, *left*, accentuated her fluid movements. A smiling male face balances the serious frown of the female fan. A Cherokee mask by Boyd Owle, *right*, manages to demonstrate both the ferocity and the gentle beauty of this carved and painted bear.

"*I dance for the simple joy of dancing, and for the closeness it brings my family.*"

Cornelia Bowannie, Zuni

Olla Maidens

ZUNI PUEBLO • NEW MEXICO

Though Zuni livelihood depended on farming, water was scarce. Women filled clay jars at springs, then carried them home atop their heads. The Zuni Olla Maidens formed in the mid-1900s, and today are led by graceful matriarch Cornelia Bowannie. Adorned with precious turquoise, *below*, the troupe recreates the serene yet joyous social dance steps of their female ancestors. Today, sacred salt replaces water in the beautiful jars that rest on the heads of the Maidens, *near and far left*.

In the Hands of Raven, by Norman Jackson, Tlingit

River Cane to Raven's Mask

DR. BRUCE BERNSTEIN

"*Native art expresses volumes about worldview and the relations of a people to their surroundings; its patterns, shapes, and material are direct, symbolic connections to place and history. It continues to represent both the very public expression of tribal identity and the intimate legacy of family traditions.*"

Creating art is a courageous act, for it places the artist into a realm others may see and experience. This is true for all artists regardless of culture, ethnicity, or other identifier. What makes Native art and artists unique, however, is their motivation. Native art expresses volumes about worldview and the relations of a people to their surroundings; its patterns, shapes, and material are direct, symbolic connections to place and history. It continues to represent both the very public expression of tribal identity and the intimate legacy of family traditions. The creation of "visual culture" is, in fact, one of the most powerful ways to express any community's notions of identity and purpose.

In some Native languages there is no word that explicitly relates to the creation of art. This absence speaks to both the functional nature of most made items and to the organic nature of the creative act. Traditionally, all items made by a tribe serve a purpose: to complete a task, to explain a story, or to invoke a spirit presence. Furthermore, the process of creation is a way of life built on philosophical and ethical systems that—no matter what changes may be introduced—continue to represent tradition and continuity. However, innovation in art is as "traditional" as the craft itself, and those who create it are among the most observant members of society, taking divergent ideas and materials and casting them into wholes that are visualized for a wider world. The role of the "Native artist" was born through just such an evolution. As non-Natives became increasingly aware of and interested in the ways that Native culture manifests itself through its objects, the skilled men and women who created those items anticipated new markets and expectations, and many began crafting items specifically for sale as art.

Since most objects throughout history were created for functionality, those who made them saw no need to sign their work. Tribes placed a higher regard on the community than on the individual, so signing artworks might have been a cultural

Northeast Algonquin groups used bark from the birch tree extensively, constructing everything from canoes to maple syrup buckets. Women carefully bit patterns into paper-thin folds of the bark, creating symmetric floral designs in a friendly competition, *above*. Today, only a handful of artists still practice this delicate art form.

"*Though these arts traditions sometimes accommodated outside market interests and tastes, they still embodied the physical and spiritual landscape of the tribes that fostered them.*"

aberration. However, as Native artists' individual recognition grew within and outside of their communities, signed pieces acquired added value. For example, Maria Martinez, the revered potter from San Ildefonso Pueblo in New Mexico, only began to sign her pots at the encouragement of non-Indians, so they could distinguish her work from that of others. By 1923, she and her husband Julian were signing all their pieces, a practice today employed by all Pueblo potters.

Native-made clothing, containers, and tools became art when outside markets realized their value, and when those who created such pieces realized that they could generate income. For example, the birchbark biting done by women of the Northeast tribes, particularly the Cree and Woodland Ojibwe nations, evolved as a means of communal entertainment. By folding thin layers of birch bark, and then biting the layers with their eyeteeth, women created pleasing designs that were later used as patterns for quillwork and beadwork. The advent of paper products nearly rendered birchbark biting extinct until it was reinvigorated in the 1990s. Known as birchbark biters, these artists mainly sell their bitings as art pieces.

The California "basket craze" is another example of this shift. In the late 19th and early 20th centuries, creating made-for-sale baskets was one of few available Native-based livelihoods, when the production and purchase of Indian arts and crafts became part of the tourist trade. Some non-Natives viewed the collecting of California Indian baskets as saving a dying craft. Traditionally, most elaborately twined or coiled California baskets were buried or burned when their creator passed away; hence, the art of basketmaking was passed down within families, but not the baskets themselves. Few early 19th-century baskets survive, which led some to believe that baskets needed to be "saved." Although this view proved incorrect, artists from the Washoe, Panamint-Shoshone, Mountain Maidu, Pomo, Cahuilla, and Paiute tribes, for example, responded to outsider demand. Between 1890 and 1930, they produced woven masterpieces created specifically for this new art market. When more European-Americans flooded California, many Natives used baskets as barter items, sparking the "basket craze." The Victorian fashion of owning Native-made baskets further encouraged the market, which flourished until World War I. The economic hardships of the Great Depression nearly ended the fashion of collecting baskets, and it was not until the 1970s that non-Native interest in the art of basketmaking was revived.

Though these arts traditions sometimes accommodated outside market interests and tastes, they still embodied the physical and spiritual landscape of the tribes that fostered them. For example, using the substances from the landscape from

which First Person was made imbues objects with sacredness. Although new tools and techniques inform the process and new markets embrace the product, Native art continues to encompass indigenous motivations. It is situated within vast reservoirs of stories, knowledge, and circumstance. Thus the use of steel tools to carve the magnificent masks and heraldic poles and house posts of the Pacific Northwest Coast does not detract from the meanings of the symbols. Art as a living entity continually evolves, yet it carries the same meanings and speaks with the same strong, clear voice.

Art continues as a critical means of self-expression and representation today. At times it has been the only form of expression allowed to Native people, who require moral and cultural contexts to make art. Today, Native artists continue to be motivated by both tradition and innovation. Tradition is still a strong force in inspiring Native artists' creation of objects that resonate with their families and communities. Interwoven within this fabric is the way that Native innovation has been influenced by other worlds. Contemporary people create art in all media while expressing multifaceted identities, including whether they are first Native people or artists on a world stage. Each object combines tradition, innovation, and art, but emphasizes them differently according to each artist's choices and

Yokuts basket-weavers of central California used a range of materials for coiling and twining their baskets. Here, a woman weaves with the coil technique, sewing a sedge weft over bundles of bunchgrass, *above left*. Images of linked human figures decorate the interior walls.

Lucy Telles, a Mono Paiute/Miwok basket-weaver, stands with her largest and most famous coiled basket in 1933, *above right*. Measuring 40 inches in diameter and 20 inches in height, the basket showcased Telles' command of form and design.

"*Interestingly, it is the contemporary production of art and craft that keeps tradition and knowledge bases vital.*"

Maria Martinez of San Ildefonso Pueblo in New Mexico carefully removes her pots from the fire, *above*. She and her husband realized that by lowering the firing temperature, their pots would achieve a lustrous, black-on-black finish. This innovation informed their designs, which borrowed from rock art and ancestral motifs.

aesthetics. Art is a negotiated space between the Native and non-Native worlds, just as it is between myriad Native worlds that continue to intersect. Interestingly, it is the contemporary production of art and craft that keeps tradition and knowledge bases vital. Native communities have a long history of interacting with many different physical and social environments, as well as adapting to new ideas, materials, and circumstances. This ability has allowed Native people to survive—physically, culturally, and spiritually—even against overwhelming odds.

Often Native peoples' motivation in keeping traditions alive is simply that these practices work and demonstratively connect people to heritage, family, and place. They remain an important way to convey information about oneself at home, at powwows, or in the outside world. Tradition and knowledge now are carried in the making of the objects, as well as in the finished piece. The only thing we can say with certainty about tradition is that it keeps changing. Making the piece creates the connection from past to present, and present to future.

In this world of Indigenous art, care must be taken in looking for differences. It is tempting to view Indian art as a barometer of cultural change (using words like contemporary, modern, and traditional), which is to neglect its value as a mechanism to maintain Native patterns and worldview. Art is not the proverbial "window" into another culture, but rather the dwelling itself. For example, coiled into a Laguna Pueblo clay pot are layers of knowledge: where to go to gather the sacred clay, and how to prepare it; how to speak to the clay (as it is a living thing), as well as how to coil, fire, stone polish, slip, and paint it. Within each step reside stories and histories, representing the voices of countless men and women who have evolved over generations from workers into artists. New pots are literally held together with ground-up sherds from pots created long ago and gathered in nearby ruins; without them, the new pot's walls would not be as strong. Thus, though what is seen may be a simple clay pot used to store water or mix dough, or even made for sale, what remains is much greater than the object itself. In essence, it is a culture's symbols made tangible and its voices rendered visible.

A strikingly beautiful circa 1900 Pomo basket is captured partially completed, *right*. The Pomo wove equal numbers of twined and coiled baskets, an unusual characteristic among California's highly developed basketmaking tribes.

A Master of Her Craft

Born in the dusty adobe village of San Ildefonso in the 1880s, Maria Martinez is recognized today as the greatest American Indian artist of the 20th century. Born Maria Montoya, Martinez quickly learned the Pueblo craft of polychrome coil-pot construction as a girl. In 1904, she married fellow artist Julian Martinez, and the two followed the Pueblo tradition of husband-wife collaboration, creating and decorating gorgeous polychrome pots, prayer meal boxes, and jars. Together, they revolutionized the way Indian pottery was viewed by the world.

The designware that would make them famous resulted from their experimentation with the potting process, such as altering firing temperatures. The couple soon perfected pottery with glossy, jet black backgrounds and contrasting matte designs. Maria coiled and stone-polished the pots, and Julian applied the design. Maria's mastery, evidenced by thin, perfectly symmetrical, and exquisitely polished work, earned her a reputation in the Southwestern art market and beyond. Because Pueblo culture values the success of the community over that of the individual, Maria steadfastly referred to her success as a shared effort. In her eyes, this demonstrated her culture's notion of ownership: her achievements as an artist were a product of the rich communal experience of being Tewa, a San Ildefonso Indian.

From Earth to Olla

To create this unique pottery, locally gathered clay is coiled and then dried, scraped, painted with an iron-rich slip, and burnished to a high shine with a smooth river stone, *above top*. The artist uses a yucca brush to paint a matte overlay, then fires the pots, which oxidize in a smothered fire, transforming the red clay to a lustrous black. Hot jars are handled with long sticks, *above bottom*. The results are beautifully subtle: Julian's beloved eagle feather motif forms a shimmering ring on a plate, *left*, while an *avanyu*, the horned water serpent, glides around a classically shaped olla, *right*.

Breathing Life into Clay

PUEBLO TRIBES • SOUTHWEST

Pottery is a central feature of the Pueblo world. It ties ceremony to function and nature to social life. For hundreds of years, these functional objects have been carefully crafted and decorated, imbuing the items—including ollas, canteens, seed jars, and bowls—with a unique power and spirit. Pueblo potters are highly respected in their community, both for continuing the ancient art form and for creating sacred vessels. Creating the pots is a ritualistic process from start to finish, a way to breathe life into clay. Ceremonial pottery still carries a "spirit break," a thousand-year-old tradition in which a painted line is intentionally interrupted. The spirit break has many interpretations, including associations with female fertility, health, and water.

Acoma's Exalted Matriarch Potter

Jagged angles form energetic harmony in this circa 1962 pot by the famed Acoma potter Lucy Lewis, *above*. Lewis is admired for her black on white fine-line hatch designs, which were partially inspired by ancient Anasazi pottery. Nearly invisibly to the eye, her patterns swell and recede according to the contours of the pot.

A Fine Form

To the trained eye, Pueblo design styles are quite distinctive. Two Zuni pots display patterns typical of the pueblo, with a banded design around the neck and around the belly, *left top and middle*. As early as 1860, Zuni potters painted deer figures pierced by a red arrow, symbolizing the heartline. Zia pots are strong, tempered with ground basalt.

Though roadrunners are typical, this pot features what may be a stylized parrot, a motif common to the region, *left bottom*. Santo Domingo Pueblo potters are known for their large ollas and dough bowls; this older example has been repaired with a buckskin thong, *above*. Such a bowl would have been used to make bread dough for feasts.

A Universal Language

Roxanne Swentzell's clay figures hum with a powerful energy akin to that which radiates from the artist herself. As the daughter of artists at Santa Clara Pueblo, she used clay as her medium of expression, and today, she works also in bronze. Though many of her figures and themes are Native, her work transcends race and gender. Her figures are characterized primarily by their humanity, conveying the irrepressible range of human emotions. To create her clay figures, Swentzell coils the heavy clay in a manner similar to that of traditional Santa Clara Pueblo potters. She begins with the bodies, which are hollow, and then adds arms, legs, and, last, an expressive face. The pieces are polished, left for weeks to dry, and then kiln-fired.

Creating Balance

Swentzell's work explores the nature of opposites, which is a fundamental theme in Pueblo ideology. In *Rope Clown*, *far right*, an inquisitive Pueblo clown examines his own dual identity symbolized in a twisting rope. Clowns, known also as *koshare*, cross social boundaries, and their light and dark stripes symbolize life and death, night and day, and male and female. This piece reminds one of the balance needed to create harmony in life. A woman contemplates the fruits of her labor in Swentzell's bronze *Admiration*, *above*. Like so many of Swentzell's figures, this woman is full of joy.

*You clay people
who dance through
my soul
dance right on
through me.
My eyes
look upon you
out there
I know you in here.
Like children
out in the world
I send you
and
hope
you find love
out there.*

Roxanne Swentzell, Santa Clara

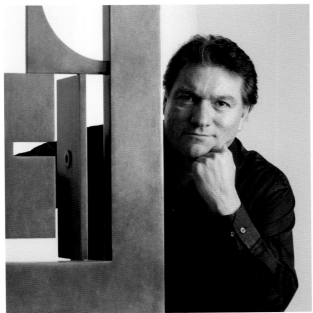

A Family of Pioneers

An artistic eye and a refusal to be pigeonholed led Tewa potter and artist Nampeyo to revive and expand the ancient Sikyatki style of pottery designs. In the 1890s, she became inspired by symbols found on sherds from the Sikyatki village ruins near her home on Hopi's First Mesa. Nampeyo, *near left top*, began to paint polychrome designs reduced to their basic, abstracted forms in a style that has since been likened to Cubism. She also revived the low, wide-shouldered style of bowls found at the ancient village. After gaining national fame, Nampeyo trained many of her family members in the craft: her granddaughter and great-granddaughter created a modern Hopi pottery style, and her great-great-grandson, Dan Namingha, *near left bottom*, is an internationally recognized sculptor and painter. Inspired by artists such as Rothko and Pollock, Namingha's work unites the spare energy of abstract expressionism with the physical and spiritual landscapes of his Tewa/Hopi heritage.

"Among other objectives, I hope to convey an appreciation of beauty, a reverence for the natural world, and a respect for Native cultures and sensibilities."

Dan Namingha, Tewa/Hopi

Personal Vision

Though more than one hundred years separates this circa 1900 bowl by Nampeyo, *right*, from her great-great-grandson Dan Namingha's *Antelope and Deer Migration*, *left*, the similarities are striking. Both use traditional Tewa and Hopi symbols with strong, bold lines and movement, balancing sharp angles with graceful curves. Like much of Namingha's work, this energetic piece combines features of the landscape—the deer and antelope—with powerful *kachina* spirit messengers.

Towering Totems

TRIBES OF ALASKA AND THE PACIFIC NORTHWEST

Originally an important part of the potlatch ceremony, totem poles were once carved and raised to represent family-clan kinship systems, stories, and accomplishments. These sculptural narratives often stood alongside the entryway to a family's home, or adorned a village as a freestanding tribute to a momentous occasion or the clan's revered ancestry.

Skillfully brought forth from cedar by a chief carver and his apprentices, a totem's animal and human forms act as symbolic characters to tell the totem's story. The story begins at the base of the pole, where the chief carver creates the intricate, highly detailed figures—often the most important characters in the tale. Apprentices then carve to the distant top of the pole, where their handiwork is less prominent. Carvers often cap the totem off with an emblematic flourish that signifies the story's conclusion. Over time, the meanings of many symbols have been lost— many, in fact, were the private artistic creations of the carver and thus never meant for widespread communication. Some themes, however, have endured and are still recognizable today, such as Fog Woman's "invention" of salmon, *near right*, which provides a cautionary tale against taking nature's gifts for granted.

Tlingit Kadjuk Bird Pole

This totem pole, *near right*, depicts Raven and his wife, Fog Woman, who called forth the first salmon from the mouth of a spring. The labret in her mouth distinguishes her as a woman of high status. The two faces that appear below the fish are those of Raven's slaves, who assisted in the creation of the first all-important salmon.

Tlingit Halibut Totem Pole

Halibut and Bear share space on this Tlingit pole, which stands in Totem Bight State Historical Park in southeastern Alaska. Halibut is easily identified by the two eyes on the top of his head. This pole honors the Halibut House people of the Nexadi clan, and was carved by Nathan Jackson to replace an original that had deteriorated with age.

Tlingit Raven House Post

Donated by Chief Saanaheit of Old Kasaan in 1901, this house post would have been placed in the corner of a large plank home. The notch in its top would have supported a large log beam that in turn held up the roof. This house post may refer to a story in which Raven captures the sun, stars, and moon for all humankind.

Saxman Native Village Totem Pole

A face resembling a bear shows its teeth on this totem pole from Saxman Native Village in Ketchikan, Alaska. Its colors are quite different from those the Tlingit usually used. Instead of vivid reds and blues, the totem pole is covered in white, black, and a nearly turquoise blue. The pole may honor Chief Ebbit, an important Tlingit leader.

Silent Storytellers

Totem poles were often wrongly identified by early European traders and missionaries as objects of worship. Today, the cliché "low man on the totem pole" perpetuates a misunderstanding of how totems function, for images carved closest to the ground are often the most honored. Indeed, the power of all the motifs stems from their enduring relevancy to important cultural stories. A human face, *far left*, seems nearly alive with emotion, while a thunderbird, *near left*, appears ready to take flight. A Tlingit *Gaanaxadi* raven crest pole, *right*, may refer to the story of Raven, who finds himself trapped in the belly of a large whale and must be rescued by villagers. Carved by Nathan Jackson and Steve Brown in 1983, it is a vivid reproduction of a 1903 pole.

Thriving Symbols

Like music and dance, art plays a vital role in the perpetuation of American Indian history and culture. Today, many Native artists simultaneously pay homage to tribal traditions and invigorate their fields, defining and challenging what it means to create art.

The Tlingit artists Nathan Jackson and Preston Singletary work in cedar and glass, respectively, infusing old symbols with new life. Because traditional wooden totem poles decay easily, few examples from before the 1800s exist. Nathan Jackson's incredible totem carvings, many of which are re-creations of historic poles, provide a living link to history. Preston Singletary, on the other hand, creates hand-blown, sand-carved glass art pieces that fuse traditional Tlingit motifs in a fragile, yet permanent, medium.

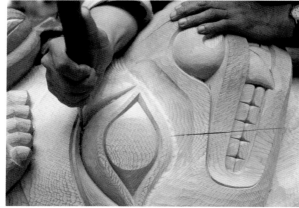

A Tradition Revived

Renowned carver Jackson, *left*, is a leader in the renewal of Tlingit totem art. Jackson carves and paints in the manner he learned from his uncle and grandfather more than forty years ago, and his totems, many of which stand proudly in Saxman Village, Alaska, show his skill with color and form. Perfectly shaped ovals are a hallmark of Tlingit totem art, *above*, and Jackson is known as a master of the difficult-to-carve shape. Working out of his Saxman Village studio, he teaches woodcarving and design classes to pass on his knowledge.

"Representing Tlingit designs in glass felt like a logical next step to me, and glass gives the work permanence."

Preston Singletary, Tlingit

An Adaptation in Glass

Preston Singletary's glass eagle glows in the light, *left*, as does his modern take on a bentwood box, *below*. This combination of Tlingit iconography and form with contemporary glass is a modern reclamation of Tlingit history using a medium that began centuries ago with the arrival of glass trade beads.

Ledger Drawings

PLAINS TRIBES

Prior to the 1850s, the lives of warriors and chiefs were pictorially chronicled on hides, rocks, and tipis, until peaceful and violent contact with European-Americans transformed many aspects of Plains life. Warrior-artists gradually adopted new methods, drawing on paper in ledgers and notebooks, and using pencil, ink, and colored pencils. For many chiefs interned by the federal government in the 1870s, ledger drawings were an innovative means to record personal and tribal conflicts, conquests, and the difficult process of assimilation. Today, many view ledger drawings as an important stepping-stone into the Native practice of fine arts. Contemporary artists such as Arthur Amiotte and Michael Horse frequently incorporate these drawings into their own interpretive artwork.

A Rhythmic Line

Bright colors and a sense of movement distinguish the ledger drawings of Sans Arcs Sioux Chief Black Hawk, *left*. The figures in *Wah-Chee-Pe, Festival Dance of Males and Females* wear trade clothes and kerchiefs as well as traditional regalia. The drawing was one of seventy-six in a ledger book completed between 1880 and 1881. When the book appeared at auction in 1994, the art world embraced Black Hawk's work, which had remained virtually "undiscovered" for more than a century. His work is unusual both for its evocative style and for its subject matter—unlike many chiefs working in ledger books, he recorded scenes from everyday life, including nature scenes, dances, and spiritual encounters. Today, the chief is recognized as one of the great Native artists of the 19th century.

Strength of Motion

Plains culture has a strong warrior tradition. Good warriors defended their people and the land, exhibiting traits of bravery and virtue; their deeds were often the subject of ledger drawings. A perfect example is a circa 1884 crayon-and-ink ledger drawing by Lakota artist Red Dog honoring the valor of a warrior named Low Dog, *left*. A highly unusual drawing by Sioux Chief Black Hawk, *above*, deviates from ledger drawings of the era. Written on the page are the words *Dream or vision of himself changed to a destroyer and riding a Buffalo Eagle*. Instead of the typical image of a warrior on horseback, a horned rider—also called a Thunder Being by Plains tribes—rides a horse-like animal

with eagle talons and buffalo horns; the creature's tail forms a rainbow that represents the entrance to the spirit world, and the small dots may represent hail. The powerful, spiritual scene demonstrates the breadth of the art form. The contemporary artist Michael Horse (of Yaqui, Mescalero Apache, and Zuni descent) takes the practice one step further by painting evocative images over copies of important documents. In *Prayer for Peace*, *right*, a holy man named Medicine Pipe sends forth a prayer, carried to the Creator by an eagle. The U.S. Constitution provides a striking, politically charged backdrop to the brilliantly hued figure and the soaring bird.

We the People

of the United States, in order to form a more perfect Union, establish Justice, insure domestic Tranquility, provide for the common defence, promote the general Welfare, and secure the Blessings of Liberty to ourselves and our Posterity, do ordain and establish this Constitution for the United States of America.

Article. I.

Section. 1. All legislative Powers herein granted shall be vested in a Congress of the United States, which shall consist of a Senate and House of Representatives.

For more than 700 years, the cliff dwellings of Mesa Verde were home to the Anasazi, an innovative people who flourished in the Four Corners area. They carved majestic buildings out of stone canyon walls, grew crops, and created a rich ceremonial and artistic culture. These first ancestral pueblo-dwellers are today known as the Basketmakers due to their remarkable skill in the craft. They used split willow in a coiled, spiral twill

technique, and waterproofed cooking baskets with pitch. Later, female Basketmakers became adroit potters, decorating their black-on-white utilitarian ware with personally meaningful designs. Though Mesa Verde was abruptly and mysteriously abandoned in the 13th century, the Anasazi left behind the seeds of an artistic legacy that continues to inspire modern descendants of the region, including the Hopi, Navajo, and Pueblo tribes.

Emerging Mediums

Between the 1930s and the 1950s, American Indian artists working in the fine arts made radical departures from traditional Native styles. These artists saw no conflict between their status as artists operating on a national or global scale, and their membership in their own tribal communities. Their work helped shape the modern and contemporary art movements, as they cast a critical eye on earlier treatments of Native life and culture. Many Native artists, including Allan Houser, T. C. Cannon, Bill Soza, Fritz Scholder, Lloyd Kiva New, and Jaune Quick-to-See Smith, used abstract imagery and bold colors to explore and explode long-standing clichés about the Native experience.

The Chiricahua sculptor Allan Houser and the Caddo/Kiowa painter T. C. Cannon are recognized as two of the most successful artists of their generation. Their pieces, though vastly different in tone and form, share a commitment to truthfully reflecting the profound changes their generation experienced.

A New Presentation

To T. C. Cannon, the political and social climate of his era could not be ignored. Works like *Mama and Papa Have the Going Back to Shiprock Blues*, *left*, determinedly avoid the romantic past of the Indian. In this case, a Navajo woman dressed in traditional fashion wears sunglasses. In the 1960s and 1970s, during which Cannon created his most pivotal works, many in the art world and beyond began rethinking their attitudes toward American Indians. Though he passed away at the young age of thirty-two in 1978, Cannon's work animates the complex range of what it means to be an American Indian.

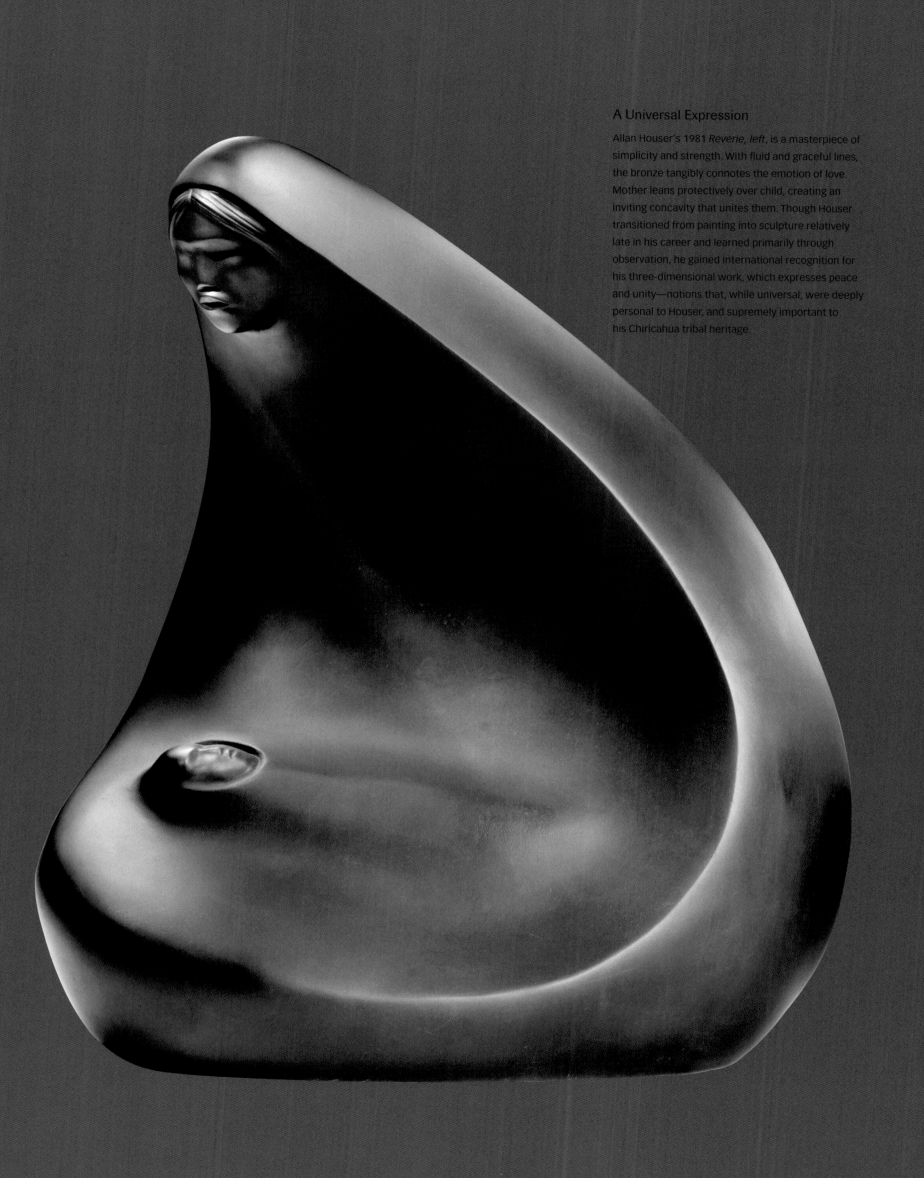

A Universal Expression

Allan Houser's 1981 *Reverie, left,* is a masterpiece of
simplicity and strength. With fluid and graceful lines,
the bronze tangibly connotes the emotion of love.
Mother leans protectively over child, creating an
inviting concavity that unites them. Though Houser
transitioned from painting into sculpture relatively
late in his career and learned primarily through
observation, he gained international recognition for
his three-dimensional work, which expresses peace
and unity—notions that, while universal, were deeply
personal to Houser, and supremely important to
his Chiricahua tribal heritage.

New Techniques

The award-winning Tohono O'odham artist Terrol Dew Johnson learned to weave baskets at the age of ten. An activist and major proponent of reviving his culture's artistic traditions, Johnson also investigates the parameters of the form with ingenious results, as in this woven gourd, *below*.

"I have learned much from my elders about tradition, patience, and technique. I combine this respect for tradition with my own visions of the world I see around me. Many times I dream a design, and it haunts me until I actually weave it."

Terrol Dew Johnson, Tohono O'odham

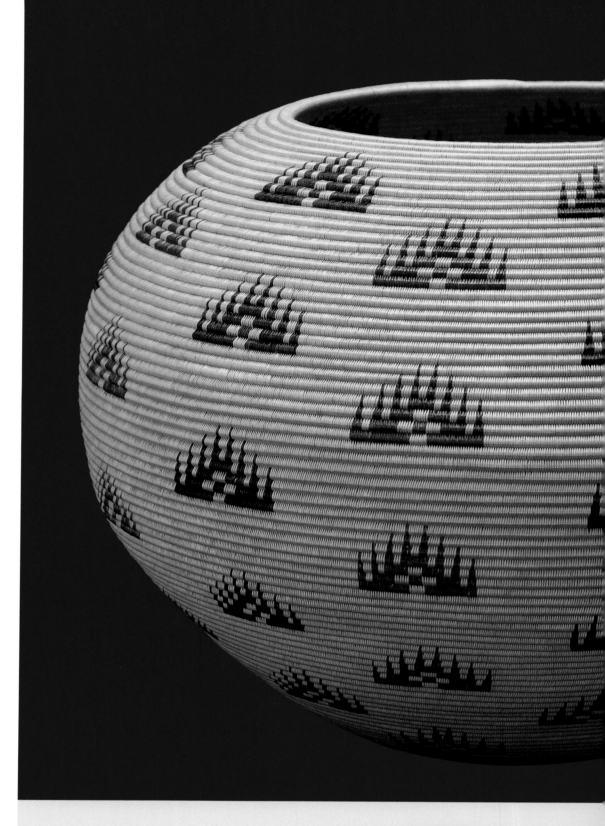

From a Whale's Mouth

Tightly woven ebony Alaskan baskets, meticulously crafted from whale baleen and topped with ivory carvings, *near and far right*, show incredible attention to detail. This rare art form is labor intensive, as baleen—keratin plates up to twelve feet long that act as filtering combs from a whale's mouth—must be trimmed, polished, and soaked in boiling water or urine to soften it for weaving.

Woven Splendor

The meditative art of basket weaving is intertwined in nearly all American Indian cultures. Like most traditions, weaving combines utilitarian function with resplendent form. Baskets were usually woven from locally gathered plant matter and decorated with geometric and pictorial images symbolic to the tribe. In the past century, individual basket-weavers such as the Washoe artist Louise Keyser have gained recognition. Born in 1850, Keyser spent more than a year weaving *Beacon Lights, left.* Comprising more than 80,000 stitches, the basket made of willow, western redbud, and bracken fern root supports her reputation as one of the best Native North American basketmakers who created for the tourist market.

Hair of Mother Earth

Braided sweetgrass and black ash splints form this unique, spherical basket made by the Iroquois artist Florence Katsitsienhawi Benedict, *above.* The perfect globe represents Mother Earth and all that she sustains. Benedict hand-gathers the tall and fragrant sweetgrass in late summer for her baskets.

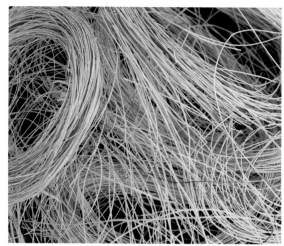

"My mother-in-law taught me this ancient art form. I've been practicing it for twenty-six years and, though I can't collect the roots and cane myself anymore, I still enjoy it."

Rebecca Bigwitch, Cherokee

Cherokee Cane Baskets

Crafted from river cane, white oak, or honeysuckle, Cherokee baskets are tangible links to a living past. Skillfully woven by women of the tribe, these pale yellow shoots are accented with boiled dyes made from bloodroot, walnut root, butternut, or yellow root, all of which are indigenous to the Great Smoky Mountains. Traditionally, Cherokee baskets were used to store food, catch fish, or even serve as gambling bean-dice shakers. The artist Rebecca Bigwitch of Cherokee, North Carolina, carefully weaves with white oak splints, which form the sturdy inner structure of the baskets. She can complete a basket in four hours—from coiled base, *left*, to finished product, *above*.

An Intricacy of Feathers

Glossy abalone and clamshell disc beads, black quail feathers, red woodpecker feathers, yellow meadowlark feathers, and the emerald feathers of the mallard adorn these ceremonial Pomo baskets, made between 1890 and 1910 for the tourist market, *above and right top and bottom*. Red and green trade beads are woven directly into the sedge root fiber walls and bottom of one basket, *left*. Women weavers of the Northern California tribe once trapped the rare birds for their gorgeous plumage; today, nontraditional game birds can be substituted, but chemically dyed feathers are never used. These exquisite baskets were once given to honored tribal members at a birth, marriage, or death, or used as currency; today, Pomo weavers mainly craft their baskets for sale.

 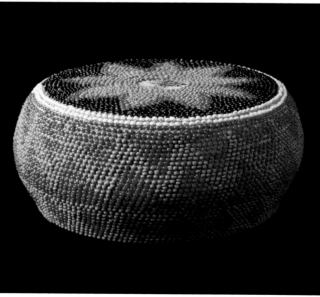

Tsegi: Spider Rock, by D.Y. Begay, Navajo

Thread the Needle

EMMA I. HANSEN • PAWNEE

"*Contemporary dance clothing and accoutrements echo centuries-old traditions and serve as powerful expressions of tribal cultures, histories, and experiences.*"

For many tribal members, attending a contemporary powwow is an unforgettable experience. The proud dancers, resplendent in their regalia, show originality of design while staying true to traditional form. Male Northern Plains dancers wear magnificent eagle feather bustles, porcupine and deer hair "roach" headdresses, bone breastplates, and beaded moccasins, and in full regalia they are reminiscent of the 18th-and 19th-century warrior society dancers. Through their gatherings, these warrior society dancers once sought spiritual protection in warfare and commemorated their personal deeds and tribal victories. Contemporary female traditional dancers move more slowly than male dancers, making the long fringes of their buckskin dresses and cloth shawls sway rhythmically. Their subtle movements symbolize the grace and power of females in Plains society, and recall older times when women stood outside the dance circle, keeping time with their feet as the men danced.

Contemporary dance clothing and accoutrements echo centuries-old traditions and serve as powerful expressions of tribal cultures, histories, and experiences. Many of their antecedents—animal hides and early reservation-era trade-cloth dresses and shirts, moccasins, leggings, eagle feather bonnets and bustles, ornaments, and accessories—reside in museums and private collections, kept as examples of the exquisite artistry and creativity of American Indian people. They reflect much more than artistry, however. The items were created for both secular and spiritual uses, and were derived from the environments and life experiences of those who created them. In these articles, we can also see the adaptations and innovations of Native peoples throughout their histories. Specifically in the sphere of women's arts, 18th- and 19th-century Great Plains women who painted, quilled, and beaded for their families and communities responded to changes in material, design inspiration, and interactions with other tribal and non-Native cultures.

A Cheyenne woman uses a quill smoother on a finished piece of quillwork, circa 1902, *above*. Cheyenne women learned the spiritual craft in a special guild under the tutelage of other women.

"*Perhaps the greatest shift in material and design was the introduction of the glass bead by European-American traders.*"

Plains women took great pride in creating beautiful and functional clothing for their families from the skins of buffalo, deer, elk, antelope, and other animals. They worked long hours thoroughly cleaning, scraping, tanning, and softening buffalo hides to create warm robes for bedding and clothing. After tanning, they embellished the hides with distinctive designs using pigments, porcupine quillwork, and glass beadwork. Before the introduction of commercial dyes, hides were painted using earth pigments and other natural materials such as blue clays, hematite for red, lake algae for green, charcoal for black, and buffalo gallstones for yellow. Ground into fine powders, the ingredients were mixed with water and thin glue made from boiled hide scrapings, which helped the paint hold its color.

Commercial pigments became available through European-American trade in the 18th century, and were widely used by Plains people by the end of the 19th century. Paints were applied using reed brushes or porous pieces of buffalo bone. Sharpened points of bone left fine lines, while rounded tips were used to color larger areas. Hide painting was one of the few art forms practiced by both men and women. Women specialized in geometric designs that reflected features of cultural life, while men recorded their successes in hunting and war in pictographic drawings.

Women also decorated clothing, moccasins, robes, and ornaments with porcupine quillwork and sometimes split bird quills. They created geometric and floral designs by flattening and dyeing the hollow quills, and then wrapping or sewing them onto the hides with sinew. Traditionally, quills were dyed with natural plant dyes, but once European-American trade goods became available, other more vibrant colors were created with aniline dyes or by boiling quills with strips of brightly dyed blankets. Hidatsa, Mandan, and Arikara artists preferred to cover blanket strips and men's clothing, pipe bags, and other items with the vivid red, yellow, orange, and violet dyes they obtained from the Fort Berthold traders.

Perhaps the greatest shift in material and design was the introduction of glass beads by European-American traders. Pony beads and then smaller seed beads became widely available, and quillwork—which was much more labor intensive—declined except among the Lakota and the Mandan, Arikara, and Hidatsa of North Dakota, who continued to quill well into the 20th century. The earliest trade glass beads, arriving to the Plains in the early 19th century, were pony beads, so named because they were transported across the Plains on horseback. At 3 to 4 millimeters in diameter, these beads were large and irregular in shape, and came in a limited range of colors, primarily black, white, and blue. They gave birth to a new art form, however, and early pony beads appeared on many items. These early designs were simple, usually broad bands or blocks of single colors in basic geometric shapes.

By about 1850, smaller glass seed beads (approximately 0.5 to 2 millimeters in diameter) in a dazzling variety of colors were readily available through long-established trade networks and centers of trade. Men and women often traded hides and surplus crops for the beads. Smaller beads were prized because they could be combined in more intricate geometric designs, and this seemingly minor difference revolutionized the art form. As women mastered the technique of beading with the tiny beads, a diversity of tribal styles and motifs flourished. Distinctions of design became markers of tribal identities. For example, Kiowa and Comanche women of the Southern Plains excelled in the fine processing of the hides and created clothing that they decorated with simple designs, such as a single motif or narrow beaded bands along the edges. The Lakota, in contrast, favored more heavily beaded materials, particularly during the early reservation period encompassing the years 1880 to 1920. During that time, Lakota women fashioned elaborately beaded dresses, moccasins, and other attire for dances, ceremonies, and other formal events.

Beads and commercial dyes were not the only new materials introduced during the 19th century. Artists experimented with items brought by traders, including cloth fabrics, tin cones, brass bells, and silk ribbons. They combined these elements with beads and quillwork, and also invented new symbols and design motifs. Lakota and Cheyenne women began beading representational images of animals and of warriors on horseback wearing flowing eagle feather bonnets. Images of the American flag, cows, and cowboys became common. Women

Horses and their Flathead riders are outfitted in glorious regalia in a 1900 photo, *above*. The cradleboard was attached to the saddle pommel of the horse on the left, while the horse on the right wears a decorative beaded collar.

"*Smaller beads were prized because they could be combined in more intricate geometric designs, and this seemingly minor difference revolutionized the art form.*"

Drawings of Plains bead patterns, *below top and bottom*, show the sharp angles of geometric form and the flowing curves of floral designs. Geometric motifs often referred to a concrete object, such as a tipi or stars, though their meanings shifted among tribes and over time.

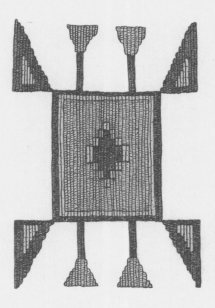

artisans also designed and beaded cradles, adult-style clothing for their children and grandchildren, and unique fully beaded pants and vests for boys. Such clothing signified to others the women's artistry and her devotion to family members.

Increased interaction with other tribes also revolutionized Plains art forms. Much of this interaction was forced, as many tribes were made to relocate to reservation territories. When tribes from the Northeast and Great Lakes regions were moved to reservations in Indian Territory, they brought with them floral designs that then influenced Kiowa, Otoe, and other Plains beadworkers. Fabrics with floral patterns also may have inspired organic beadwork designs. Once settled on reservations, Plains women continued to produce exquisite works of art. It has been suggested that they did so simply because they had easier access to trade materials and more leisure time without the traditional time-consuming duties associated with the buffalo-hunting way of life. Another interpretation, however, is that these artistic styles were created during difficult times during which Native people met seemingly overwhelming challenges to their physical and cultural survival. For them, art became a means of expressing and renewing their cultural heritages because of, and despite, the adversities of the late 19th and early 20th centuries.

Artists have always had integral roles and responsibilities within Native communities as providers of both secular and sacred materials, recorders and interpreters of cultures and events, and visionaries of the future. They have long adapted materials and technologies to produce multilayered works that were functional and relevant to cultural and spiritual lives. Contemporary artists—now equally men and women—use "traditional" methods such as hide work, porcupine quillwork, and beadwork, and infuse them with new ideas and experiences. In this manner, these earlier art forms and the ingenuity of past artists are carried into the present. Today, artists like the Choctaw beader Marcus Amerman create new artists' mediums; he uses beads to create stunning, politically-charged portraits of American Indians and re-creations of historic tourist postcards. Debra Box creates and paints rawhide parfleche envelopes and boxes in the style of her Ute heritage, curing the hides and mixing the earth pigments herself, with stunning results. As artists, they—and many like them—continue to preserve cultural identities while meeting new challenges of contemporary life.

A feathered headdress like this circa 1900 Teton Sioux example, *right*, was worn by a prominent warrior. Each feather was given by a war veteran along with a story that proved the warrior's right to own such a glorious treasure.

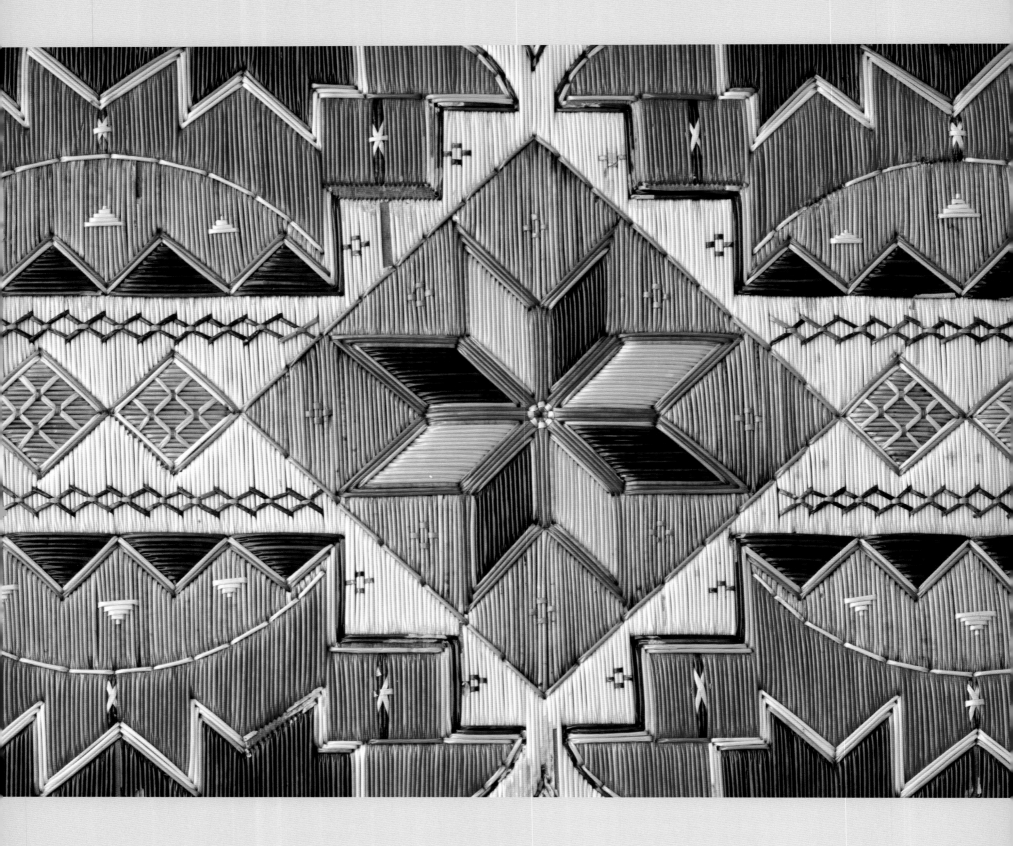

A Quill's Progression

A close look reveals the mastery required to transform quills into beautiful designs. Once quills were stripped from the porcupine, they were sorted by size. Large tail quills adorned work bags, while smaller quills, more difficult to work with, decorated special pieces. In order to be used, quills had to be softened, split, and dyed. The Omaha, for example, used saliva to make the stiff quills pliable, flattened them with their fingernails, and then colored them with dyes made from roasted yellow earth and cottonwood buds. Quills were usually stitched onto rawhide, birchbark, or animal hide tanned with brain. Micmac patterns were first designed on folded sheets of bark or hide and used as templates, which were traced with sharpened pieces of bone. Awls made from bone, sharpened antler points, or thorns pierced the backing. The pointed, barbed end of the quill made a natural needle, and was threaded through the small holes. Other tribes affixed the quills to the hide with loops of threaded sinew. Delicate patterns similar to those in embroidery were laid out with exact precision in groups of parallel rows, or fanned out in diagonal star shapes, *above*.

Technical Perfection

TRIBES OF THE PLAINS AND THE NORTHEAST COAST

The ancient art of quilling was women's work, a highly respected and sometimes sacred craft that was widely practiced before the advent of glass beads. Quillwork societies trained and honored those women who had mastered the time-consuming and complex techniques needed to create quillwork, for unlike other art forms, technical precision was valued over artistic innovation.

Beautifully stitched quilled boxes by the Micmac of the Northeast set the standard, *below*. By the late 19th century, Eastern tribes created purses, cases for plaques and portfolios, and other useful items to satisfy the European tourist market, *near left top to bottom*. Some impressively decorated boxes require more than 10,000 dyed quills.

The Challenge of Creation

An expert craftsman, Amerman creates both texture and shadow in his beaded images. A tribal man in Southwestern attire focuses intently on his work in *The Beadmaker* (2003), *below*. The striped blanket upon which he sits resembles the striated layers of a mesa, while a subtle white radiance behind the man's head conjures up a Byzantine halo or a sun. The contemporary use of beadwork to recreate a traditional image is an intentional—and interesting— opposition. Though Amerman was raised primarily in Oregon, he spent childhood summers in the deserts of New Mexico; the blending of many rich cultural traditions is reflected in his work.

Updating an Historic Form

For the Choctaw artist Marcus Amerman, shimmering glass beads speak a language more nuanced than floral or geometric designs can express. Inspired by the colorful beadwork of the Plains and Plateau tribes, Amerman creates intricate portraits, as meticulous and exacting a process as that of traditional beadwork. It is there, however, that the similarities end. Amerman's work reveals his critical, and often humorous, eye for social commentary, frequently taking aim at stereotypical imagery of American Indians and blending pop art motifs with Native themes.

In his 1997 portrait *The Man with No Name, left,* Amerman depicts the annonymous stoic Plains warrior who captivates the imaginations of so many non-Natives. *The Gathering, above,* captures the duality of worlds many Natives straddle. Set against a dramatic mountaintop, a group of mounted Indians in traditional dress are silhouetted against a thoroughly modern skyline. Amerman assumes an outsider's perspective in order to present a worldview that juxtaposes Native and non-Native art forms.

Touching the Earth

The icon of American Indian footwear, the moccasin was once ubiquitous from Maine to Alaska. Most were sewn from one or two pieces of tanned hide, and Plains tribes often used a tough rawhide sole. Northeastern tribes typically had a puckered U-shaped vamp over the top of the foot, while Alaska Native tribes lined their *mukluks* with fur for added warmth. Subtle distinctions in material, symbols, and bead or quill decoration distinguished tribal affiliation at a glance. Like other items decorated by Plains tribes, quilled moccasins became less common as seed beads were used as embellishment. Everyday moccasins had little or no adornment; beaded moccasins represented a labor of love and deep respect, and were usually reserved for special occasions or ceremonial rites of passage.

Elegant Presentation

Pueblo tribes rarely if ever used beads; the Zuni Pueblo moccasins, *far right bottom*, are instead painted in vivid shades of red, yellow, and green. A pair of Otoe moccasins from Oklahoma, *near right bottom*, displays scrolling floral beadwork and a side-flap construction typical of the Southern Plains. Blackfeet moccasins, *near right top*, are heavy with geometric beadwork, which is attached to the hide in a "lazy-stitch" design style. Green cloth adorns the cuffs and nicely accents the delicate beadwork of an historic pair of Huron or Wyandot men's moccasins, *far right top*.

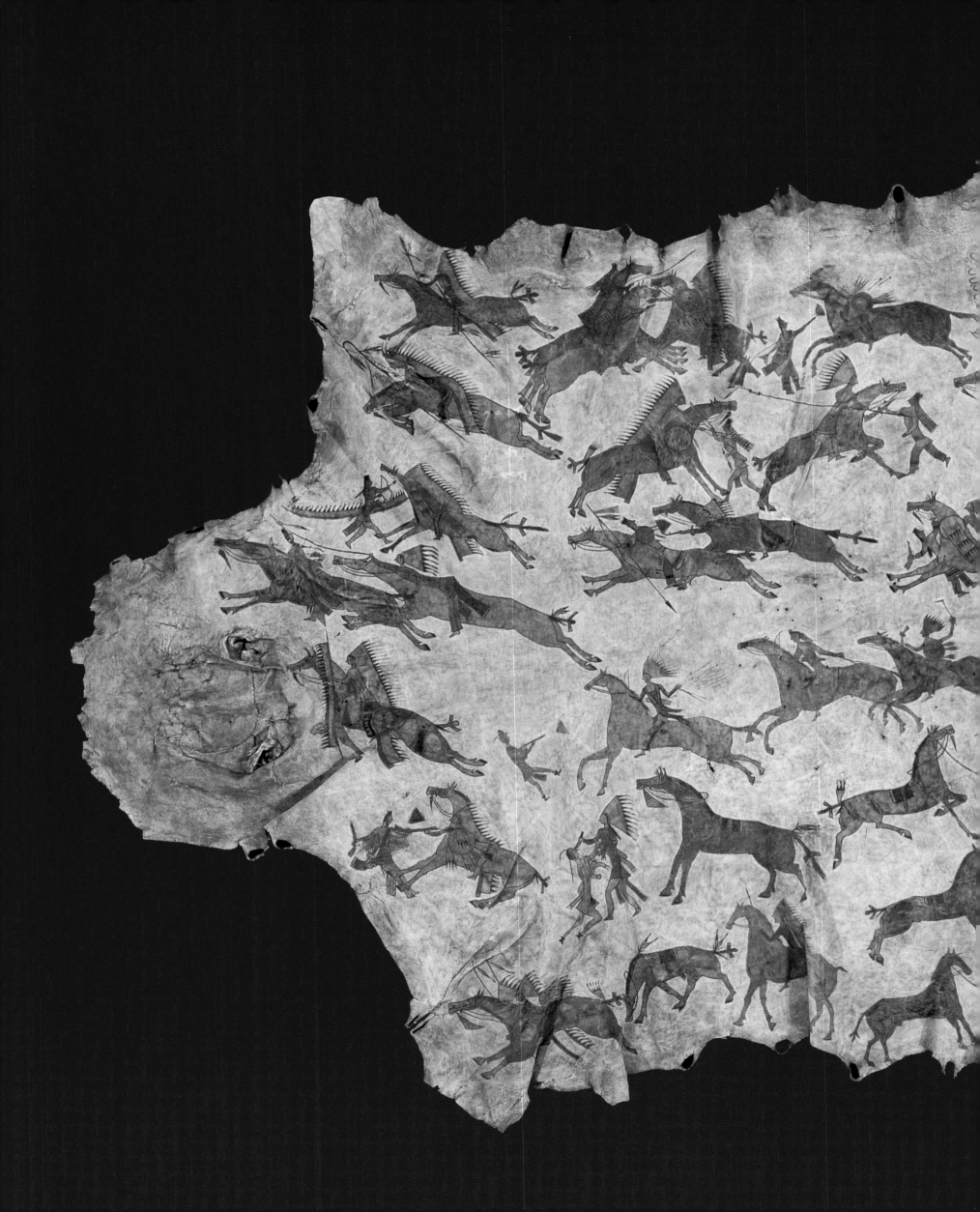

History Captured on Hide

PLAINS TRIBES

Among the Plains tribes, pictographic depictions on hide played an important role in historical and cultural preservation; war records and winter counts were two common forms. War records, such as the circa 1880 Teton Sioux painting, *left*, identified distinguished warriors and chronicled their battlefield prowess in vivid color and movement. Winter counts were similar to calendars, and were used to pictorially record pivotal events in a tribe's history. For example, one record's image told of "the year the stars fell," which was later identified by scholars as the Leonid meteor shower of November 1833.

"Big Missouri" Winter Count

Kills Two, a Brule Sioux medicine man, paints the "Big Missouri" winter count around 1923, *above*. As new materials became available, winter counts and war records were copied onto muslin or paper to preserve them.

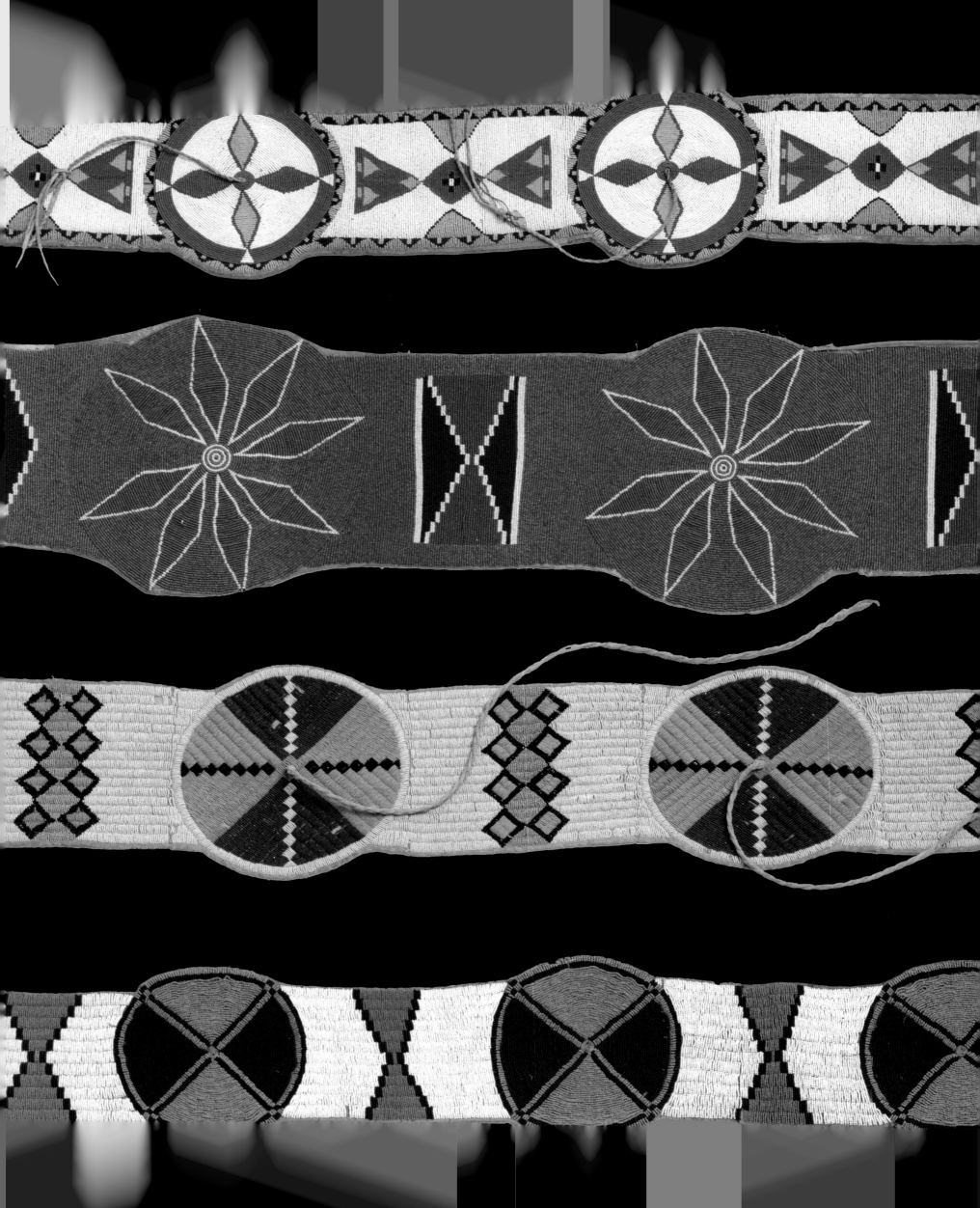

Beaded Blanket Strips

Though stone and bone beads have been used by tribes for more than 10,000 years, glass beads were incorporated into Plains artistry only 150 years ago. So valuable were the sparkling beads that, at one point, a horse could be traded for one hundred beads. The uniform shapes and exotic colors of beads allowed new techniques and styles to develop, including elaborate blanket strips, some of which are more than six feet long.

These early 20th-century blanket strips made by Assiniboine, Pawnee, Nez Perce, and Sac tribes, *left top to bottom*, testify to both patience and technical expertise. Created to adorn the back of a buffalo- or elk-hide robe or a trade blanket, and cover any center seams, the beaded masterpieces were hung vertically down the back of the wearer. The blue and red rosette of the Pawnee strip, *below*, is larger than a man's hand. For Plains Indians, a woman's dexterity in traditional arts earned her honor and dignity within her tribe.

Blanket Stories

For the artist Marie Watt, of Seneca heritage, wool blankets are the markers of one's life. People sleep intimately curled around their blankets; blankets are also symbolically meaningful to many Native communities. Despite the disease-riddled blankets donated by non-Natives in the 18th century, blankets play a largely positive role in tribal economy and culture. Blankets were traded for other goods, and are today still given and received as emblems of respect and honor. In Seneca tradition, women fashioned skirts from beaded wool.

Watt transforms discarded wool blankets into columnar ladders in *Dwelling, below*, evoking the towering totems of Northwest Coast tribes. *Braid's* colorful diamond patchwork, *right and far right*, recalls the historic process of quilt making and the loops in the symbol of infinity. With each piece, Watt reclaims the blanket as a source of community pride, artistry, and empowerment.

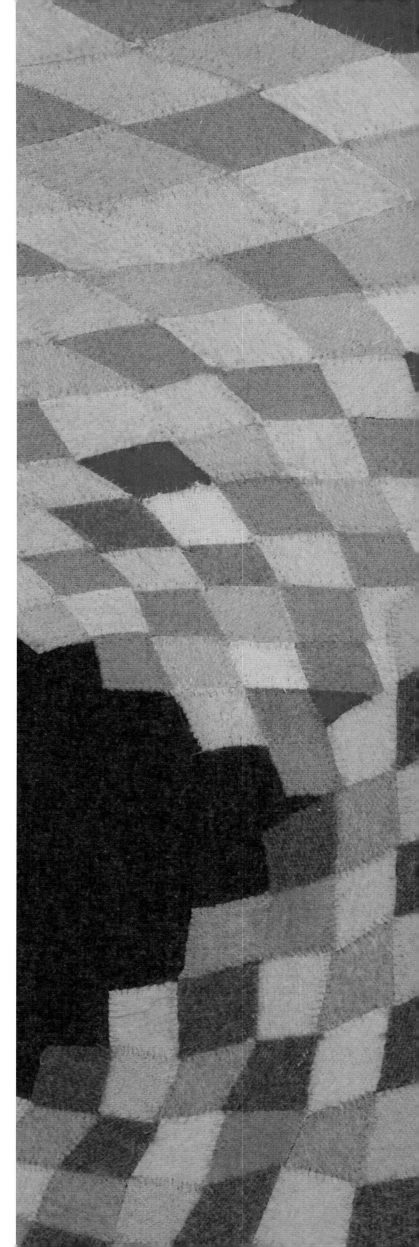

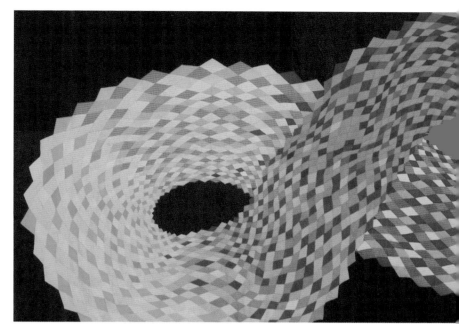

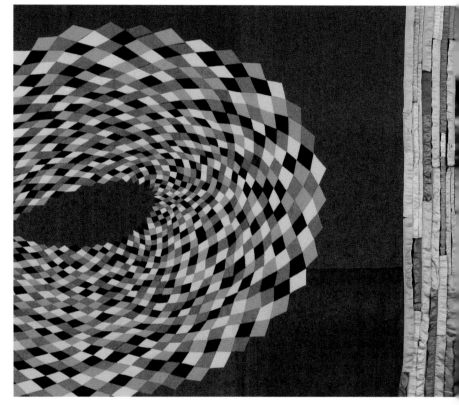

*"Blankets gain meaning through use.
My work is about social and cultural
histories imbedded in commonplace
objects. I consciously draw from
indigenous design principles, oral
traditions, and personal experience
to shape the logic of the work I make."*

Marie Watt, Seneca

Silver Works of Beauty

NAVAJO • ARIZONA AND NEW MEXICO

For more than 1,000 years, tribes of the Southwest fashioned personal ornaments from shell and semiprecious stones. In the mid-19th century, Atsidi Sani became the first Navajo to learn the art of metalwork by apprenticing with a Mexican blacksmith. Later, he experimented with silver, and a new craft was born. By the end of the century, bright turquoise inlay became common, as did finely hammered concho belts, *below*. The Navajo taught the technique to other tribes such as the Zuni, and as the Southwestern tourist market grew in the early 20th century, so did the market for expertly crafted silverwork. To this day, the Navajo are revered for how they cast, beat, stamp, or hand-work the malleable silver into distinctive jewelry.

Navajo Concho Belts

A close-up of an elaborately designed concho belt, *right*, reveals egg-shaped turquoise stones and gleaming silverwork. Navajo designs are influenced by Spanish, Mexican, and Pueblo motifs, though their beauty is all their own.

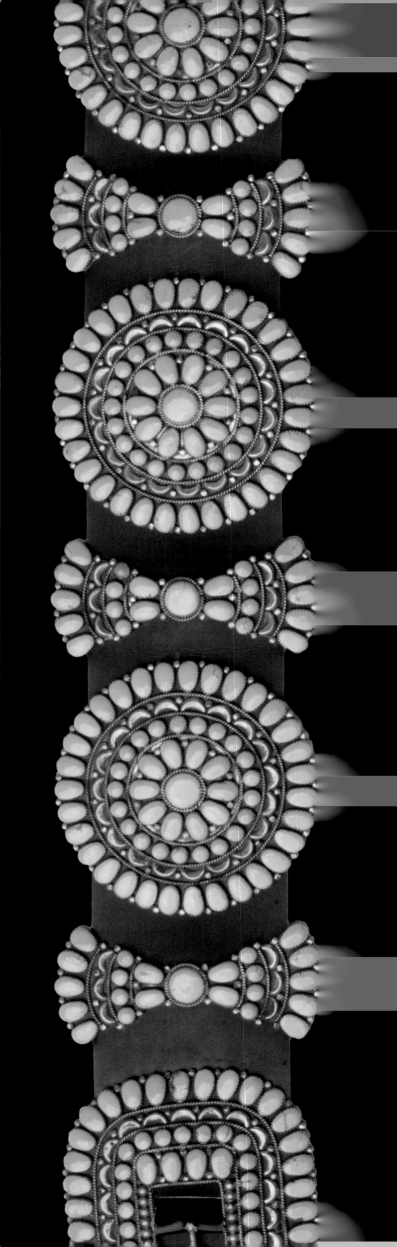

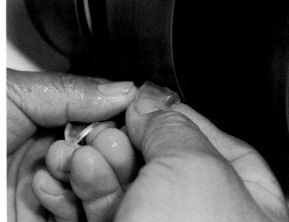

"*My grandfather said that from sunup to sundown, you should be doing something of value, and now I feel that I am.*"

Duane Maktima, Laguna/Hopi

Innovative Design

Family, spirituality, and the integrity of tradition are of key importance to the award-winning jeweler Duane Maktima, of Laguna and Hopi heritage. A longtime advocate for the traditional art forms of Pueblo cultures, Maktima founded the Pueblo V Design Institute in 1997 to provide assistance to emerging artists. His celebrated jewelry, made at a studio in his New Mexico home, *right top and middle*, fuses Scandinavian, Asian, Art Deco, and traditional Pueblo motifs using semiprecious stones, gold, and silver, resulting in unexpected combinations of color and form, *right bottom*.

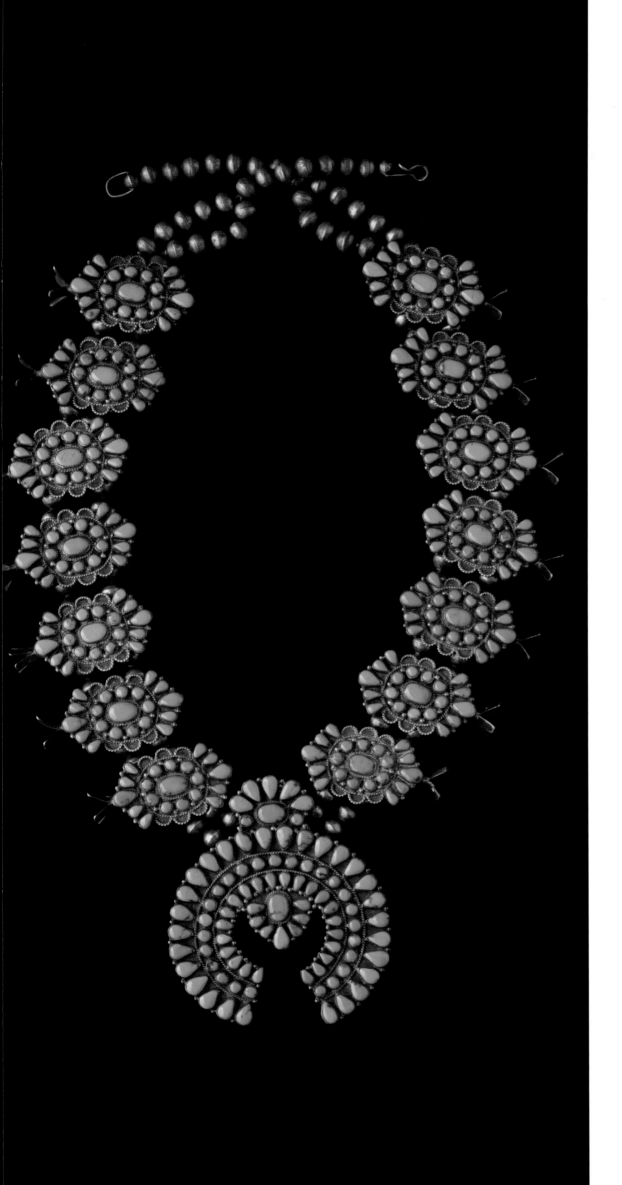

Shell to Squash Blossom

Drawing inspiration from their ancestors, Navajo, Hopi, and other Pueblo artists create an array of styles using traditional materials. An inlaid squash blossom necklace from Zuni Pueblo, *near left*, is a popular style inspired by the pomegranate shapes brought by visitors from Granada, Spain. A contemporary bracelet cuff by the late Hopi artist Charles Loloma, *above top*, contrasts coral and ivory with turquoise, while an unidentified Santa Clara Pueblo artist created a herringbone inlay pattern on shell, *above bottom*. Though at least 600 years separate an ancient Anasazi necklace from a contemporary Zuni Pueblo piece, *far left*, the two have much in common. Both used stones particular to the Southwest, as well as shell, though the artist of the mosaic shell pendant (made between 1200–1400) would have traveled as far away as the Gulf of Mexico to trade for the bivalve and shiny oyster shells.

Spider Woman's Legacy

NAVAJO • ARIZONA AND NEW MEXICO

It is said that Spider Woman and her husband, Spider Man, introduced the art of weaving to the Navajo, spinning the first web of the universe on a loom made from the sky, the earth, and its elements. Adopting the upright loom, *below*, from their Pueblo neighbors, female Navajo weavers took quickly to the craft. They herded *churro* sheep, sheared, cleaned, carded, and spun the wool, and then created textiles that are now legendary for their technical craftsmanship, bold designs, and watertight construction. Though Navajo men are learning the art form, it has been passed down from mother to daughter for centuries.

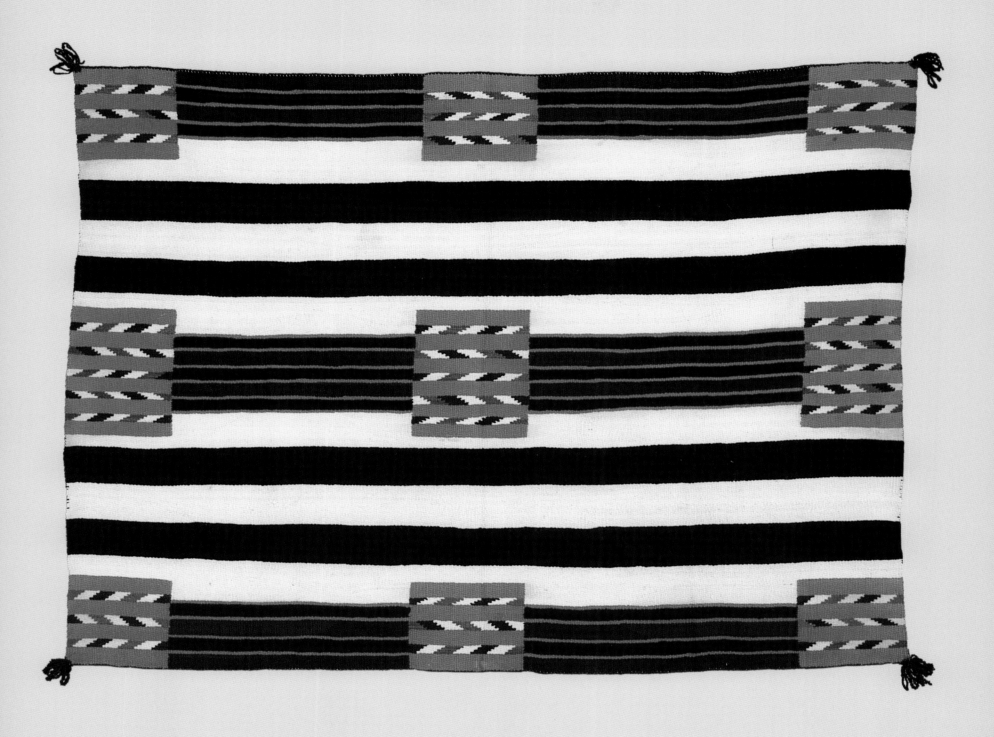

Chief Blankets

Striking lines and strong colors trace an evolution of form in chief blanket styles. Unlike many tribes, the Navajo did not have "chiefs"; however, the blankets were often given to other American Indian leaders, hence their name. The blankets are separated into three distinct phases based on their style. Created between 1850 and 1860, first-phase blankets feature brown-black, indigo, and cream stripes, *left top*. Fewer than one hundred first-phase blankets exist today, and are highly prized. Second-phase transitional forms, woven from 1860 to 1875, included wefts of red Bayeta yarn, *left middle*. Phase-three chief blankets, created between 1875 and 1900, incorporated brightly colored geometric shapes such as crosses and rectangles, *left bottom and above*.

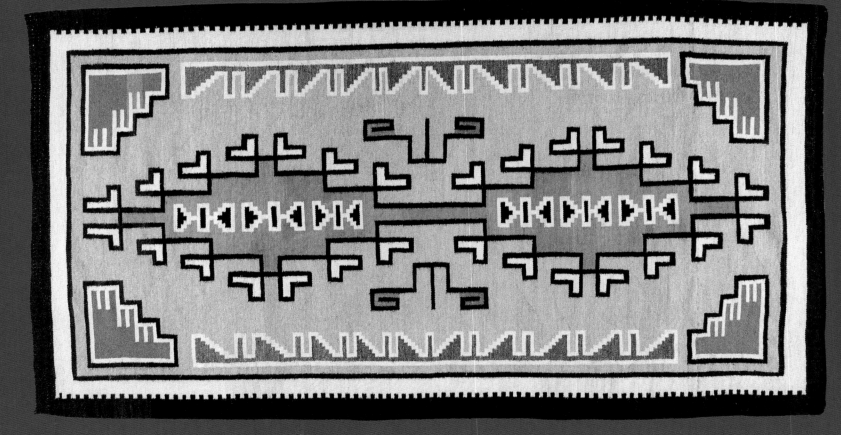

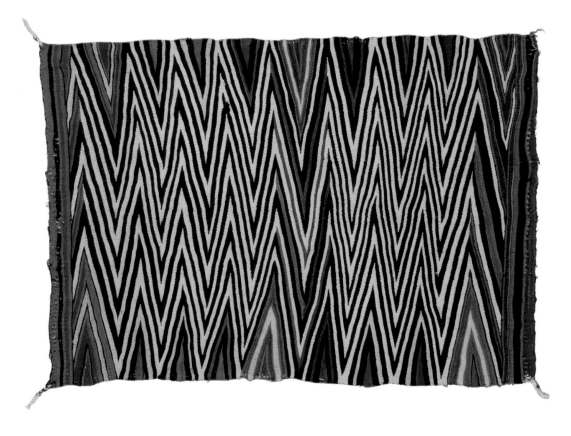

Variations on a Theme

As weavers honed their craft, they pushed the boundaries of their own creativity, challenging one another to spin the tightest yarns and to create daring designs. Weavers at the beginning of the 20th century also capitalized on the availability of commercial dyes and developing market tastes. "Eye dazzler" blankets fused the brilliant colors of Germantown wool with energetic designs evocative of lightning, *above and near left*. Non-Native trading post owners on the Navajo reservation, looking for profit, encouraged artists to develop new weaving styles. Two Grey Hills rugs, *far left top and bottom*, are known as some of the best. Their rich earth tones, a hallmark of rugs from that region, are the natural colors of the local sheep's wool. Navajo weavers continue to reach new artistic heights in the weaving industry.

Weaving As Life

Using a palette of rich earth tones, the Navajo artist and fourth-generation weaver D.Y. Begay creates innovative weavings in the tradition of her mother and grandmothers. She raises *churro* sheep, whose long, silky, black-and-white wool is best for weaving. Begay was instructed by her parents at an early age how to shear the sheep, and card, spin, and dye the wool. Begay says that spinning is the most important part of the weaving process, for producing the fine, even thread determines the quality of the rug.

"Our weaving traditions have been passed down for centuries. I began as a young girl in Tselani, because my mother always told me, 'These hands are for weaving.'"

D.Y. Begay, Navajo

A Natural Process

Begay was inspired by her paternal grandmother Desbah Nez, a dyer and weaver, and today she uses everything from black beans, bloodroots, and onion skins to prickly pear cactus and chamisa, called *diwozhiilbaih*, to make her spectacular colors, *far right and right top*. As a young girl, Begay watched her *nali*, or grandmother, collect rabbit brush to dye her rugs. Begay then watched her boil a pot of water mixed with bunches of the shrub. Undyed wool was added, and after what seemed like hours, her *nali* drew forth vivid yellow yarn from the pot. Begay repeats the process as she was taught, *left*.

Today, when Begay prepares to weave, she sits at her loom, *near right*, to begin the meditative process. She weaves classic Navajo and Ute-style rugs, as well as designs inspired by Plains parfleche, Pueblo *mantas*, and the mesas outside her Arizona home (see page 216). The results combine Begay's own personal artistic vision and the values and traditions of her Navajo ancestors.

Button Robes and Blankets

ALASKA NATIVE TRIBES

Alaska Native tribes have used the button, which flashes in the light, for more than two hundred years as decoration for woven robes and blankets. Centuries ago the robes were used only in religious ceremonies, and buttons were used only to decorate the crests centered on them. As buttons became more widely available due to increased trade, they began to be used to border the tops or sides. Traditionally, the number of button rows correlated with one's status in the community: one row of buttons indicated a child or someone of middle class, while three rows were reserved for community leaders or nobility. Four rows of buttons appear rarely on the robes of those who deserved great recognition.

Today, wool felt button robes and woven Chilkat and Raven's Tail robes are donned for dancing. Woven robes, which are rare and more expensive, are preferred. Men dance a more dynamic style, allowing the robes to flare open during turns. Women move more subtly and with quiet grace.

Regalia of the Naa Kahidi Dancers

Young Tlingit members of the Naa Kahidi Dance Group from southeastern Alaska wait their turn to dance, *far left and right bottom*. Symbols on the troupe's regalia represent their clan systems. Raven grandly spreads his beaded wings, *near left*, while an eagle strikes a regal pose, *right top*. Bright red fish swim in blue wool waters as Tlingit adults prepare to enter the dance arena, *left top*.

Fringe About the Body

It can take up to a year's work and the wool of three mountain goats to complete one intricate Tlingit Chilkat robe. These gorgeous robes were given in potlatches, traded by Northwest Coast tribes, and worn by Tlingit nobility, *above*. Traditionally, only men were allowed to design the patterns, which were often modeled after crests, spirits, or animal figures, *left*. Women then wove the robes from goat's wool and cedar bark, using dyes made from berries and minerals. Chilkat weavers are renowned for their ability to weave in a curvilinear form—the robes are the only type of weaving in the world to incorporate circles. A weaver signs her work by incorporating two small checkerboard patterns on the lower left and right corners of the robe—each signature is unique. Chilkat robes are used for dancing, as the long heavy fringe sways dramatically to the beat of the drum. In fact, the Tlingit name for the Chilkat blanket is *Naaxein*, or "fringe about the body."

Cold-Weather Gear

ALASKA NATIVE TRIBES

For centuries, the construction of seal-gut parkas, or *qas'peq*, has been an important functional art. Today, Alaska Native women still sew with sinew, mastering the tight stitches needed to make the garment waterproof, resilient, and lightweight.

Seal or sea lion intestines were cured in one of two ways. First, the gut is inflated with breath, *below,* and then split open. In summer, the sun dries the gut to a lustrous translucency. In winter months, the seal gut is dried outdoors in subzero temperatures, which renders the material opaque. Historically, parkas were worn by men on hunting trips on land or at sea, and were imperative in keeping them warm and dry.

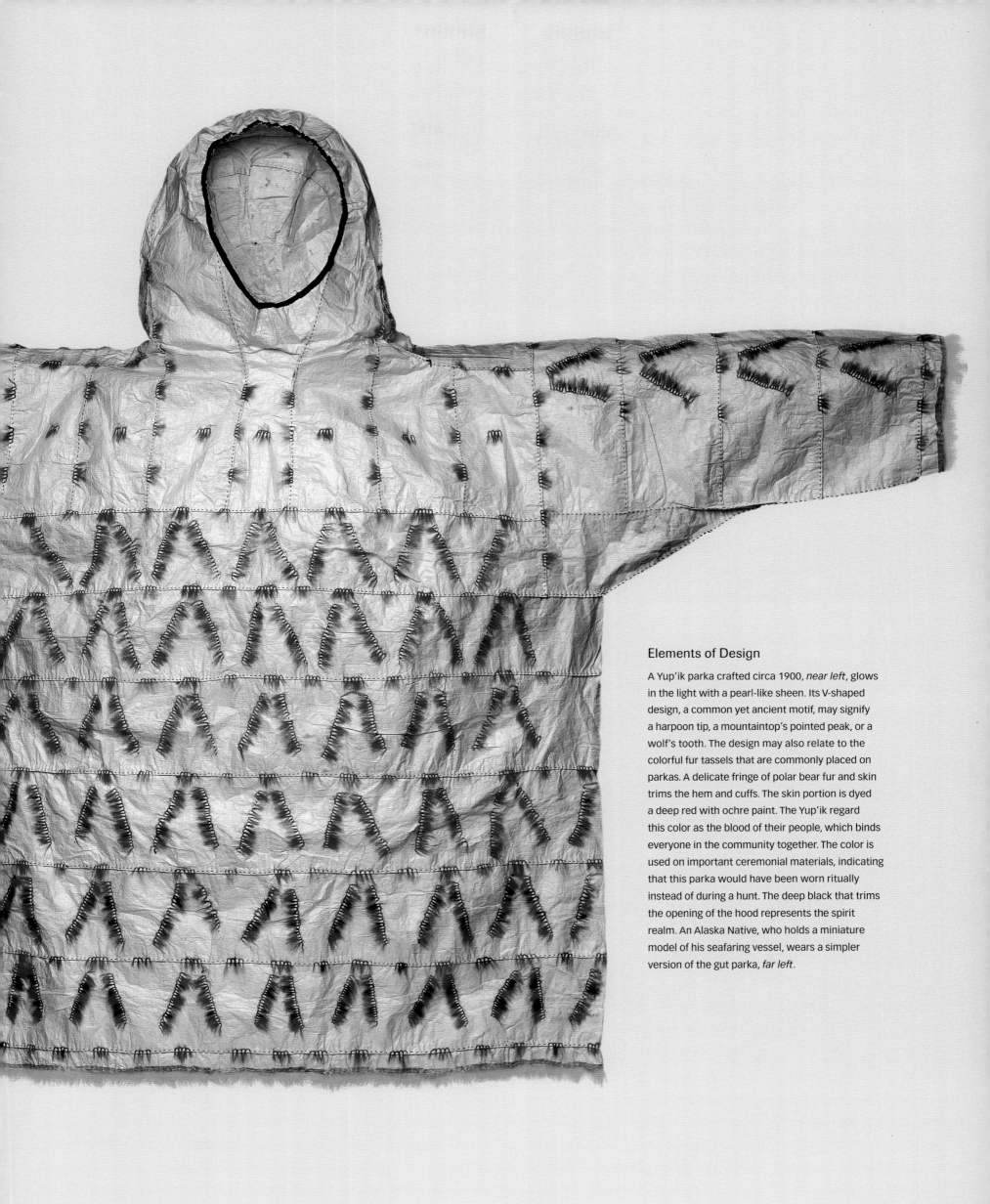

Elements of Design

A Yup'ik parka crafted circa 1900, *near left*, glows in the light with a pearl-like sheen. Its V-shaped design, a common yet ancient motif, may signify a harpoon tip, a mountaintop's pointed peak, or a wolf's tooth. The design may also relate to the colorful fur tassels that are commonly placed on parkas. A delicate fringe of polar bear fur and skin trims the hem and cuffs. The skin portion is dyed a deep red with ochre paint. The Yup'ik regard this color as the blood of their people, which binds everyone in the community together. The color is used on important ceremonial materials, indicating that this parka would have been worn ritually instead of during a hunt. The deep black that trims the opening of the hood represents the spirit realm. An Alaska Native, who holds a miniature model of his seafaring vessel, wears a simpler version of the gut parka, *far left*.

Osage Woman with Landscape, by Anita Fields, Osage/Creek

Bounty of the Elders

DR. GEORGE CHARLES • YUP'IK

"*Despite its bleak, snowy cover, the tundra teemed with flora and fauna that gave life to those who found it. All members of the family, young and old, participated and made meaningful contributions to the family's food supply.*"

Each year after freeze-up my family would move to the winter camps and hunt for furs. During this time, most Yup'ik families would take to their own hunting areas, spreading out on the snowy Alaskan tundra dotted with thousands of lakes. My father would hunt fox, mink, otter, and wolf. I would go out with him and the dog team to check the fur and fish traps, bouncing along on the sled as the dogs caught the scent of fox and increased their speed. Overhead, we would occasionally see a raven, flying on the coldest of windy days, seemingly without a care in the world. Sometimes we would see a mysterious *anipak*, or snowy owl, which is the winged carrier that shuttles messages between the Yup'ik people and animals, deceased human beings, or the land.

Despite its bleak, snowy cover, the tundra teemed with flora and fauna that gave life to those who found it. All members of the family, young and old, participated and made meaningful contributions to the family's food supply. My mother set fox traps, using partially dried salmon eggs as bait, and my grandmother twisted *yualut*, caribou sinew, into thread for stitching fur parkas. Giving feasts were held each winter when the skies were lit with the spectacle of the Northern Lights. In this manner each season passed, filled with activities tied to the land and the skills needed to survive.

Survival lessons were taught in never-ending *qulirait*, or stories, recounted in the mother tongue. According to my elders, it was *Ellam Yua*, the Person of the Universe, who gave the power of speech to the Yup'ik when he created the first man and woman. *Ak'a tamaani*, translated "a long time ago in that place," is a phrase that begins most Yup'ik stories, used by all fluent storytellers. For me, this phrase is synonymous with being Yup'ik. Some stories related to hunting and gathering, human and animal behavior, or the seasons. Others taught one to observe the environment, using examples of trial and error to emphasize the importance of

Well-made wooden fish traps were essential to life, and Yup'ik men were masters of their craft. Beautifully woven traps such as the black fish trap, *above top*, and the larger version, *above bottom*, were built to last, ensuring that families—such as these Central Yup'ik children and their father—could survive long winters.

survival skills. Acquiring food took much energy and time, and the windows of opportunity to do so were narrow. Starvation was an ever-present threat, and stories of our ancestors' conduct in the face of adversity were retold at every opportunity. Through these tales, we learned to balance our time between gathering plants and hunting, always in reference to the seasons. Food gave you the energy and life to carry out the rules of living and its related ceremonies. The community's survival depended on these life-giving endeavors.

One tale in particular demonstrates these close connections to land, ceremony, and story. The people of Nunacuaq suffered from tremendous hunger one year when the run of the white fish, the mainstay of their diet, did not return. In the white fish's absence, the seemingly unimportant but bounteous black fish helped the people survive the winter. To this day, some women descendants still sew a symbol of the black fish tail onto the back tassel of their *atkuq,* or parkas, to commemorate the occasion. Such symbolic rituals of respect for animals or plants are common; passed on by precontact elders, these customs are still celebrated today. Inspired by such gestures, younger tribal members are reclaiming some of these rituals, like giving a drink of fresh water to a seal after it has been killed or giving a small fish to the land as an expression of thanks.

My life as a Yup'ik was formed by my parents, my grandparents, my larger family, and my community. My upbringing and my life today—*Yuuyaraq,* or the Way of the Human Being—was and is directly informed by the *qulirait* (stories) and *yuarutait* (songs) of my people. My parents were taught by their elders that words and thoughts are real, that words have power when spoken with conviction and clear intent. Feelings were also said to have power. Silence and respect were taught and instilled in the young. One did not look directly into the eyes of the elders, and the young did not initiate conversation with elders. It was proper, however, following strict protocol, to ask certain questions—especially ones regarding the acquisition of tribal knowledge. To be Yup'ik is to be immersed in the never-ending and circular *ak'a tamaani* stories that retell the relationship of all created entities in the Yup'ik universe.

In the winter nights, following the evening meal, my favorite part of the day would begin: the telling of stories by the elders, especially those told by traveling hunters staying overnight on their way up north to *Qaluyaaq,* Nelson Island. I would stay up with them as they recreated the past in the mind's eye. As a boy, I watched the young women draw pictures with their *yaaruin,* or storytelling knives,

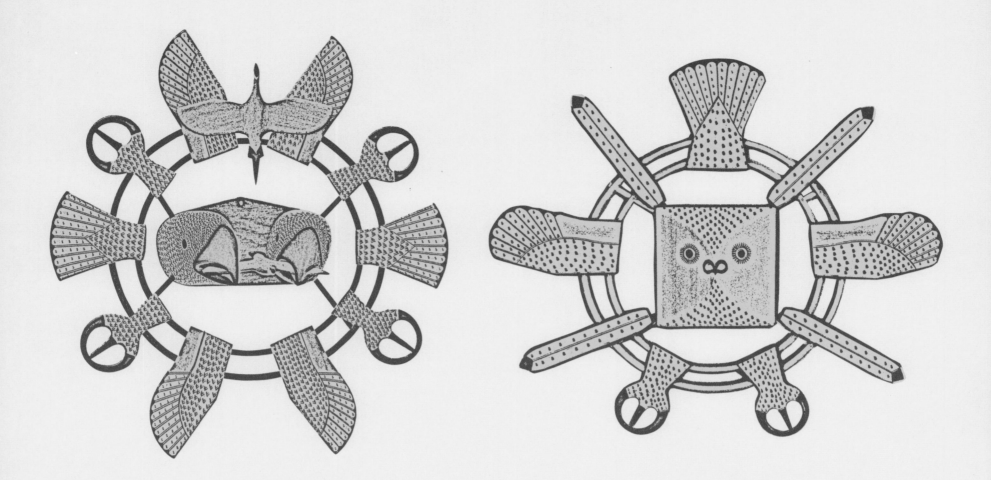

in screens of mud. They would go from screen to screen, tracing familiar images—a human figure, a house—as the story progressed. Each screen was erased by spitting on the picture and smoothing the surface of the mud with the knife. Stories told with the *yaruiq*, a knife usually made from ivory, would especially mesmerize the listeners. Such storytelling is seldom seen these days.

The male elders told many stories while they carved the various implements needed in everyday life, usually as they sat in the *qasgi*, or men's community houses. The *qasgi* were found in more permanent Yup'ik villages and were the training places for young men. At about age nine, boys left the *ena*, women's house, for the *qasgi*, where they ate, slept, sang, danced, and told stories. When my father, *Ayaginar* (which means "one who pleasantly travels"), began his training, there was no bedding, and he used his mittens as his pillow. From watching his elders— uncles, cousins, and other extended family members—*Ayaginar* learned to make hunting tools, sleds, kayaks, fish traps, spears, drums, and masks. He was given a bow and arrow and taught to hunt small birds and then ducks and geese. Young men learned patience through endless repetition, and they received constant encouragement. Meanwhile, girls in the *ena* were trained by their female elders, learning to sew, prepare food and skins, and behave as proper Yup'ik women.

Drawings of two masks carved by the author's father *Ayaginar*, also known as Nick Charles, portray a double hawk and a snowy owl, *above*. In Yup'ik tradition, the owl is believed to be endowed with the power of supernatural sight.

"As a boy, I watched the young women draw pictures with their yaaruin, *or storytelling knives, in screens of mud. They would go from screen to screen, tracing images—a human figure, a house—as the story progressed."*

Soft mink fur provides the basis for this winter parka, sewn and proudly worn by Yup'ik Elder *Nengqeralria, above,* the author's mother. White calfskin, wolf, wolverine, and beaver also adorn the coat. Parkas such as these were made for everyday use rather than ceremonial wear. She holds two dance fans crafted from driftwood.

It was also in the *qasgi* where community rituals, ceremonies, and feasts were held. My mother, *Nengqeralria* (which means "one who is pleasantly extended"), remembered seeing a *kuvyaq,* a net made of sealskin, hung in such a way that it could be pulled by a rope to move it in sync with the beat of the ceremonial drums. White feathers tied to the net represented the stars. In these ceremonies, as many as twenty drummers would play the drumheads made from walrus stomachs. When the *qasgi* was not large enough to hold all the guests, part of its tundra sod sides were opened up. My mother also remembered watching the refurbishment of her village's *qasgi* in a ritual of renewal that she referred to as the "Giving Festival." The entire community worked together to lay new logs for the floor, add wall planking, and provide a new seal-gut window. As an elder, *Nengqeralria* was one of the last true story-song singers. She was also recognized as a dancer-singer, skin sewer, and craftsperson. To her, and to my father as well, enacting the traditions that they learned in childhood was not intentional cultural preservation, but rather embodying what the Yup'ik people have always done, constantly trying to replicate the lessons learned from their elders. For this reason, my parents were nationally recognized as living treasures, imparters of sacred knowledge.

My earliest memories include wearing sealskin pants that my mother made so that I could play in mud puddles without getting wet. I remember watching my father dip for smelt on a rainy day while I was kept warm in a seal-gut raincoat. Later I set fish nets, chopped wood, gathered berries and eggs on the tundra, and learned to carve Yup'ik masks like my father. According to school records, I attended first grade twice, second grade twice, skipped third grade, and went twice to fourth grade, the longest stretch I was ever in school being thirty days. This was because my life was rich with learning on the tundra, in the rivers, and in the forests of Alaska. I am who I am today because I am Yup'ik, raised by my elders who emulated the best of the Yup'ik Nation.

This beautiful *Cauyaq* wood and gut drum, *right,* made by Yup'ik artist Tony Sonny, accompanies masked dance performances. The word *Cauyaq* means "one you look at," for, when playing the tambourine-like instrument, the drummer faced it at all times, holding it up with one hand and then reaching around the drum's back with the other to tap it with a thin drumstick.

Crow Ways of Learning

CROW • MONTANA

A tribe's long-term survival depended on its ability to train and prepare the next generations in the life skills and knowledge of their people. The ways of knowing and learning were person- and family-centered, and designed to raise children to be complete members of society. There are myriad ways to absorb information, *right*, and the ability to listen and observe was a valued talent and virtue. Very few activities were restricted to adults, and children were constantly in a rich learning environment. Elders encouraged listening and observation, and often assigned tasks to sharpen these abilities, whether spotting game at a distance, watching the horizon for movement, or picking a route along the hillside or through the prairie. Today, many of these methods are still employed by the Crow tribe as valuable tools for teaching youths.

On the Way to Crow Fair

Crow Elder Louella White Man Runs Him Johnson, *above*, leads a group to Crow Fair. Proudly celebrated for more than one hundred years, Montana's Crow Fair attracts tens of thousands of Natives who come to dance, rodeo, and celebrate the passage of time.

Methods of Knowing and Learning

- Naming traditions fall to a chosen name-giver, selected by the parents. Name-givers often become mentors to the children they name.

- Observation of nature, stars, and the seasons leads to better understanding of the surrounding world.

- "Story sticks" adorned with miniature objects accompany and illustrate oral traditions and history.

- Learning through analogy is a foundational tool of Native ways of knowing and learning.

- Grandparents and elders train cousin groups of a similar age, who learn by repeated practice.

- Tribal specialists instruct whole generations of boys or girls of a similar age in "age-grade societies."

- Vision quests and dreams, seen as directions from the Creator, provide pathways for a seeker once they are interpreted by tribal advisors.

- Grandmother's lodge is a place for learning, growing, and the nurturing of infants and young children.

- Role models instruct and engage youths.

- Trickster stories, particularly those of Old Man Coyote, relay morals through entertainment.

- Peer teaching among children helps older siblings learn the skills of teaching and younger siblings gain in expertise or knowledge.

- Pageants and reenactments, such as the War Bonnet Dance, bring the history of the Crow people to life.

- Parents arrange apprenticeships for their children with a master to acquire special knowledge.

- Children familiarize themselves with useful skills needed later in life by playing with child-size tools.

- In family workgroups, even the smallest children are assigned tasks to learn the value of group effort.

- All men and women on the child's father's side are considered clan parents, who help teach and advise.

- Intensive listening and observation of elders are valued and respected learning tools.

Honing New Skills

Crow children were often grouped with role models who were chosen by their parents to teach a particular skill, *left*. For example, young boys could be paired with an expert in arrow throwing; they would attend arrow games to learn and listen. Gradually, the child would be taught the throwing techniques through narrative, and then in practice with small arrows, *above top*.

Long winter months were a time for children to move indoors and keep warm inside the family tipi, *above bottom*, and to learn their tribe's history. Storytellers used winter counts—quilled or beaded pictographic representations that recorded major events in a family or tribe's year—to illustrate the stories and make them come alive.

The Desert People's Way

TOHONO O'ODHAM • ARIZONA

Revered for their artistry in weaving and basketry, the Tohono O'odham of southern Arizona make seasonal pilgrimages into the Sonoran Desert for yucca and beargrass to create their coiled masterpieces. These sturdy fibers are harvested in the desert in summer and winter, respectively, and provide the weft and warp of the baskets. Historically, only women gathered these plants, but today, men and women of all ages embark on collection trips to gather the precious materials. Traditionally, young girls learned the skill by watching others, and gave their first completed basket to the elder women who taught them. Tribal Elder Molly Celestine, *right*, collects yucca, *above*, to create overlay designs for coil baskets. Today, skilled female artisans are highly revered in O'odham community life, and gladly make the communal forays to gather the grasses, though they must travel farther and farther from the reservation to find them. The demands of agriculture and irrigation from nearby developments have devastated cattail and willow habitats, and even hardier beargrass and yucca now require trips as far away as New Mexico. However, such ritual journeys reflect the extent to which the land affects and inspires the tribe; in fact, the very words *Tohono O'odham* translate into "Desert People."

"My grandmother Molly has been a basket-weaver all her life. She is the reason why I fight to preserve the ways of basket-weavers and the materials needed to continue this art form."

Terrol Dew Johnson, Tohono O'odham

Yucca Gathering

Only the ends of the young, pale green shoots of the *tock-way,* or yucca, are chosen for Tohono O'odham basket weaving. Nestled in the center of the plant, *right top*, they are delicately plucked by hand and twisted in a back-and-forth motion until they break free at the base, *left and above*. Next, the bundle is shaken to release any shoots that are too short to use, *right bottom*. Remaining yucca shoots are cleaned one at a time, split, and spread on the ground for up to two weeks until they are bleached white. Just before weaving, the stiff shoots are soaked in water. Yucca collected during the winter months is usually a deep green and will not bleach white; it is used as an accent color in design.

Willow, once a preferred material, did not grow well enough in the desert to support the basketmaking industry, and yucca has gradually become the preferred foundation for Tohono O'odham basketry. These strong fibers form the bottom base of the baskets and decorate the coiled beargrass sides in both closed-stitch and open-stitch patterns. The finished walls of the baskets are pounded with stones to flatten and smooth the sides, meshing the materials together.

Beargrass Collection

Samuel Fauyant gathers *moe-hoe,* or beargrass, by hand, *above and left top and bottom.* The razor-sharp blades are twisted free and tied into bundles to be sorted and combined into thicker, longer cords. These cords are gradually spliced in to form the sides of the basket. Many baskets are so watertight they are used to hold freshly prepared saguaro cactus wine during the annual *Nawait,* or Rain Ceremony, to invoke rain for a successful harvest. Today, bundle-coiled baskets are most commonly produced. When open-stitch artistry is employed, often in the form of stars and sunrays, the soft green of the underlying beargrass contrasts beautifully with the other materials that adorn it.

Bone-white yucca and soot-black devil's claw (another local plant) are woven over and around the deep green beargrass to create innovative and striking designs that include animal figures, fret patterns, and plants and stars. *I'itoi, right,* from Tohono O'odham cosmology, appears prominently in the "man in the maze" motif. The image symbolizes the many choices humans make in their lives, growing wiser but drawing ever closer to death, as portrayed by the dark center.

ᎤᏃᏍᏗᏍᎩ ᏪᏍᎢ

Sequoyah's Legacy

CHEROKEE • OKLAHOMA

Language is a lens that brings the world into focus, allowing us to describe what we see to others, especially those perspectives that are unique to a culture. Language is also a vital measure of a society's well-being. For these reasons, the Cherokee Nation goes to great lengths to preserve its language, called *tsalagi*. Today more than 10,000 people speak and write it fluently.

There is a great tradition of spoken Native languages, but written language is a rarity. The Cherokee syllabary, which was first developed by Chief Sequoyah in the early 1800s, has been an invaluable tool in establishing *tsalagi* as a writing system. Similar to an alphabet, a syllabary is composed of syllables instead of letters. For instance, the symbol "ⱺ" stands for the sound "nv," and "Ⱡ" stands for the sound "da"; together, these two syllables create "nvda," the Cherokee word for both sun and moon. The syllabary is so indispensable to Cherokee identity, and so aesthetically powerful, that its emblems often find their way into art, as in *Hunt Well* by the noted Cherokee artist America Meredith, *left*.

ᎠᎦ ᎤᏛᎠᏒᎠ ᏣᏯ ᏔᏗᏍᏆᏐᎢ. ᏌᎩᏱᎮᎷ ᎦᏬᏂᎯᏍᎦ ᏕᏍᎭᎠᎠᎠ ᎠᏔᏫ ᎤᏁᎶᎠ ᏔᎩᏁᎡᎢ ᎡᎩᏯᎮᎷᎡᎵ ᏣᏯ ᏕᏍᎭᎠᎠᎠ ᏔᏎ ᎢᎦᎢᎠᎢ ᎠᏔᏫ. ᎤᏂᎭᎡ ᏌᎠ ᎳᏫᎶᎭ ᏅᏚ ᎶᎠᎡ Ꭱ ᏒᏗᎩᏈᎡᎢ ᎩᏯ ᏔᏗᎡᎢ ᎠᎠ ᎤᏒᎢ ᏌᎠ ᎳᏫᎶᎭ ᏍᏍ ᎩᏯ ᏔᏗᎡᎢ ᏒᏗᎩᎶᎡᎢ. ᎲᎠᎢ ᎢᎡᎳᏟᎵ ᎩᏯ ᏕᏍᎭᎠᎠᎠ ᎤᏛᎠᎠᏫᎢ.

Transliteration

Do-yu u-li-s-ge-di tsa-la-gi tsi-di-wo-ni-s-go. Yi-gi-yo-hu-hi-se-lv ga-wo-ni-hi-s-di a-tsi-la. U-ne-tla-nv-hi i-gi-ne-lv-i da-gi-yo-hu-hi-se-li tsa-la-gi ga-wo-ni-hi-s-di i-ga go-li-go-i a-tsi-la su-na-le yi-nu-la-s-da-ni nv-da di-ka-lv-gv e-di-yo-li-ho-i tsa-la-gi i-di-ho-i a-le u-sv-i yi-nu-la-s-da-ni s-quu tsa-la-gi i-di-ho-i e-di-yo-li-hv-i. Ni-ga-v tsi-ni-da-dv-ne-ho tsa-la-gi ga-wo-ni-hi-s-di u-tlo-ya-s-do-i.

Translation

Language is really important. If we lose the language, we lose the fire, because the fire only understands Cherokee. In the morning, we rise and greet the sun in Cherokee, and at night we greet the darkness in it. Everything we do is related to language.

– Hastings Shade, Cherokee scholar and descendant of Sequoyah

A Tradition Upheld

TAOS PUEBLO • NEW MEXICO

Whether nestled along cliff slopes, set atop soaring mesas, or laid out in the flat desert sands, the adobe structures of the Southwest stand out as stunning examples of architectural ingenuity. Years ago, entire Pueblo communities rallied to build these villages, molding clay, sand, straw, and water into bricks that were then sunbaked and stacked into structures. Wooden poles called *vigas* formed the framework for the roofs, *right*, while mud mortared the bricks in place and adobe plaster sealed the outer surfaces against the elements.

Today, these buildings are recognized as crucial emblems of Pueblo identity. Assembled in tight and often multistory clusters, they promote community togetherness; historically, they provided protection. Many generations have participated in their upkeep, applying layers of mud plaster every few years before major feasts. Vigorous restoration programs now emphasize replastering's importance, thus fortifying the pueblos' status as living monuments. With each stroke of the trowel, participants in the communal process secure a sense of permanence for their homes, and for their heritage.

Layer by Layer

Members of the Taos Pueblo restore the roof and walls of an adobe building located outside Taos, New Mexico, *above*. Such renovation projects tackle structural problems like cracks and bulges in the plaster and decaying wooden support beams, all of which result from the natural shifting of the adobe bricks as their water levels fluctuate over the years. These repairs are often community events, as at Chamisal, New Mexico, *left*. Elder participants instruct youths to labor by hand as their ancestors did, replastering with natural materials such as mud, clay, and straw to maintain the delicate balance of the building's original composition. They also correct water drainage flaws that could cause future fissures or pockmarks in the smooth red adobe facade. This careful attention preserves these architectural treasures for future generations.

Pueblo at Dusk

Pueblos are an extension of the earth, rising from the ground in copper-colored swells that mimic the Southwest's rock formations. This unity between geography and architecture reflects the Pueblo Indians' harmonious worldview, in which nature and quotidian life are perfectly intertwined. It also extends to religion, as the terracelike structures are based on key themes in the Pueblo belief system. For instance, according to a Pueblo origin tale, the first human ascended from the underworld to the earth's surface, and then to the heavens; hence, ladders stretch between floors and lead onto the roof, allowing inhabitants of Pueblos to emulate this spiritual journey. Crucial to tribal identity and visually striking, pueblos are chosen as subject matter by many artists, represented here by Dan Namingha's *Pueblo at Dusk, left*.

While pueblo architecture is certainly rich in symbolism, these structures are also practical. Built with natural materials and baked by the sun, the adobe walls slowly absorb and release heat. In the winter, they retain warmth from the sun and radiate it into homes as the cold night sets in. The buildings' slow absorption rate also prevents summer heat from penetrating the interior, keeping inhabitants cool during hot days.

Following in Step

Vance Beaver of the Muscogee (Creek) Nation shows his grandson Keegan the steps at the Natchez, Mississippi, Powwow, *above*. Dancers shake bustles and turkey-feather fans during the Grand Entry at the Shoshone Powwow in Wyoming, *near right*. The Grand Entry—a processional of all costumed dancers—is usually followed by a flag song and prayer. Any number of dances may then follow, ranging from informal intertribal and social dances to the more complex, often newer dances such as the Men's or Women's Fancy-Shawl, a blur of footwork that requires incredible endurance. At the Maryland Powwow, George Whitecloud Sullivan, a former Washington, D.C., police officer, crouches low in deerskin regalia, in the beginning stages of the "sneak-up dance," *far right*.

Triumphant Assembly

The contemporary powwow is more than a gathering of dancers; it is a reaffirmation of tribal culture as manifested through song, dance, language, food, and blessings. Adapted from the Narragansett word *pauwau*, which refers to the sacred, powwows evolved from the ceremonial war dances of the Great Plains. They have since spread throughout Indian Country, and play host to an increasing number of cultural activities, from pipe ceremonies to honoring of veterans.

Each year, tens of thousands flock to powwows to perform and honor their tribes, dancing both with and for one another. Many powwows offer competitions that honor innovation in dress and step alongside more traditional dances. Many dances are intertribal, meaning that participants from various regions can dance together. Talented dancers, drummers, and singers are celebrated not just for their skills, but also for the leadership and respect they bring to the event. The resonating drumbeats and dance steps, full-throated call of the singers, and flashing colors of beads, feathers, and fringe vividly affirm and celebrate contemporary Indian identity.

"*I grew up going to the powwow, and danced Traditional most of my life. Today at a powwow, you go to compete, but also to dance and meet new people. It becomes a family gathering, a place to come together.*"

A.J. Agard, Standing Rock Sioux

Rhythm of the Drum

Adam Nordwall, a Shoshone/Chippewa/Navajo dancer, in beaded regalia, watches the festivities with his daughter, *above*. Three Shoshone women at a powwow in Cody, Wyoming, gently move their fans in an up-and-down motion, *left*. Known as the Women's Northern Traditional, this dance requires smooth movement, grace, and elegance. Buckskin or cloth dresses are heavy with beadwork, and elaborate breastplates move in time to the beat. Though contemporary and traditional dances are dramatically different, both find appreciative audiences at powwows around the country.

"Some stories belong to a family, like property, and can only be told by family members. It is a powerful way to teach the next generation its history."

Gordon James, Skokomish

Keepers of the Stories

Storytellers do more than remember strings of words; they are masters and proponents of a fertile oral tradition whose very existence relies upon their abilities to recall and convey important cultural narratives. Many are closely rooted in the natural world, demonstrating a deep kinship to and understanding of the land and all life it supports, which was often paramount to a tribe or individual's survival. Such wisdom might also encapsulate a tribe's or family's history, provide practical or ceremonial information, or explain the behaviors of prominent animals. Gordon James, a Skokomish storyteller, notes that although a story's meaning could not be altered over time, the old narratives retain their power and relevancy because they speak in multivalent ways to tribal members over time. James was chosen by his tribe to learn the stories of his people. His tutor, a Skokomish elder named Subiyay, knew more than 700 stories. Today, James and his wife Pamela (of the Colville tribe), *above*, travel throughout Indian Country, giving presentations on health and wellness, and telling those stories that must be remembered.

Spoken Wisdom

American Indian stories bind communities together, illuminating the larger cycles of life. Intended to instruct, honor, and entertain, they are passed down through many generations, containing the wisdom needed to survive. Bringing these histories to life requires powerful orators, who are handpicked by tribal elders for their abilities to listen and remember the stories, some of which may last an entire winter season. Their importance is demonstrated in the joyful clay Cochiti Pueblo storyteller figure, *below*, and in the 1966 painting *Aged Tutor and Young Students* by Navajo artist Harrison Begay, *left*. From the tutor's lips, the stories of his people assume vibrant color and shape, as the next generation attentively listens and learns.

The midday summer sun casts no shadow over Sitka Sound and Baranof Island, where the Tlingit, Tsimshian, and Haida have lived since the last Ice Age. Located on Alaska's southeastern panhandle, the sound borders the Tongass National Forest, America's largest at seventeen million acres. Spruce, western red cedar, and western hemlock trees—home to eagle and raven nests—meet blue waters. Five species of salmon make

their home here, as do trout and halibut. Sleek sea otters and seals patrol the sound as well, just beyond the reach of the brown and black bears that wander through the underbrush. On what was once a thoroughfare for Gold Rush ships, today tribespeople of Alaska's Inside Passage are as likely to see cruise liners from the decks of their local fishing boats as to glimpse bald eagles and leaping king salmon.

Lessons in Tlingit

TLINGIT • ALASKA

Eight-year-old Miko Kirby, *above*, proudly displays the fruits of her labors: a bucket of ripe huckleberries, picked during *Shaanaxwéiyi Dísi,* or the moon's cycle when "berries are ripe on the mountain." Miko is one of fifteen Tlingit children spending a week at Dog Point Fish Camp, a lush 160-acre plot in the midst of the Tongass National Forest near Sitka, *right.* Founded by Koolyeik Roby and Nas.aax John Littlefield in 1988, the site is both Tlingit-language immersion school and working fish camp, and embraces the notion that since culture is embedded in the Tlingit language, it is essential that Tlingit youths learn both at once. As only 200 speakers remain in southeastern Alaska, most of them over seventy, passing on ancient lifeways and the language of the land is crucial. Youths at the immersion camp learn from fluent tribal elders, many of whom have traveled great distances to teach them. An afternoon might be spent salmon-fishing, otter-fleshing, or, for the younger kids, simply learning which red chokecherries are ready to pick.

"Our food is our way of life, and represents the way of the people."

Nas.aax John Littlefield, Tlingit

"We offer up food into the fire to remember our loved ones and our ancestors who have gone on before us. By calling out their names, we honor them, and they will be remembered and fed."

Koolyeik Roby Littlefield, Tlingit

Sea to Smokehouse

The days are full at *Waashdáanx',* or Dog Point Fish Camp, where nature's abundance provides ample opportunities to learn from elders of the Raven and Eagle moieties. Nas.aax John Littlefield holds the line-net still as Kaakdláa Adam Larson and Koonwuhaan Leonty Williams check for wriggling fish, *right*; the day's first catch of coho and dog salmon are then cleaned, filleted, and hung up to dry, *left*, by the smokehouse. The chatter of Tlingit fills the camp, where stumbling phrases are met with encouragement, laughter, and gentle instruction. Students also learn the oral history of their ancestral land, which spans thousands of years prior to the last glacial surge.

Tsu héidei shuaxtootaan, yá yaa koosge daakeit, haa jeex' anak has kawdik'eet.

Tlingit adage

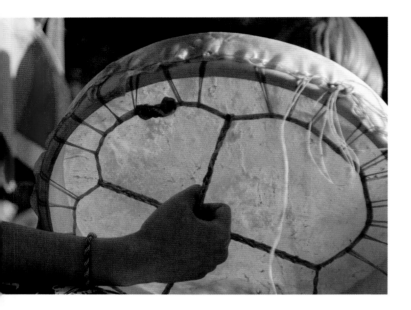

We will again open this container of wisdom that has been left in our care.

English translation

A Day Winds Down

The drum sounds often at Dog Point, *above*. Accompanied by song, drumming around a fire may honor ancestors or provide a send-off to camp visitors as they depart by boat. Through the drum's beat and the song's words, the language's rhythm is reinvigorated and passed on to the next generation. During the summer, as many as forty Tlingit youths may pass through this stunning fish camp. Each student signifies the Tlingit community's commitment to the language and the preservation of the cherished lifeways that have sustained their culture for ages. As an August evening coasts slowly into darkness, *right*, residents of Dog Point Fish Camp prepare to turn in for the night. Even the dog salmon, for whom the point is named, have ceased jumping. Sitka Sound is still.

Map of Featured Tribes

This regional map locates those American Indian tribes, bands, reservations, and tribal communities featured in this book.

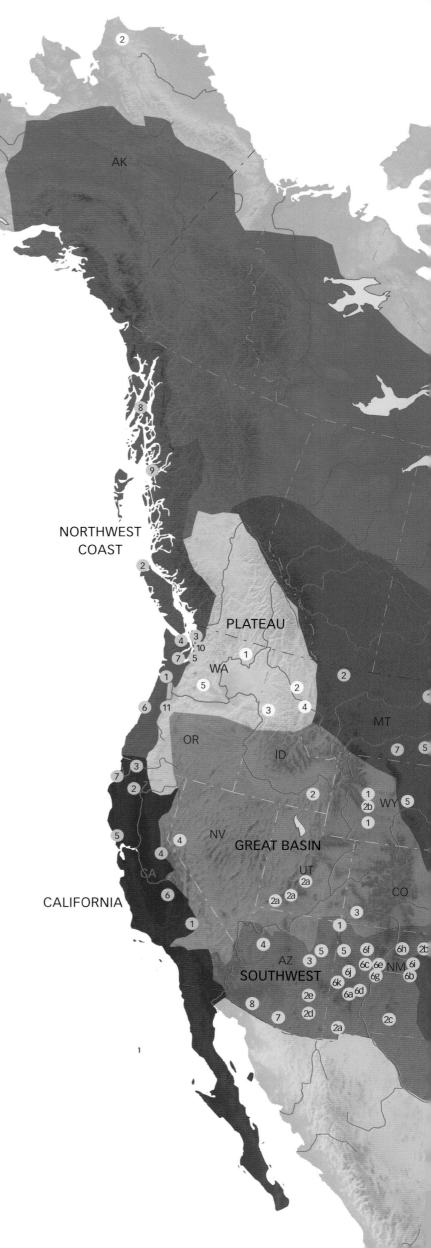

ARCTIC

1. Ingalik
2. Inupiaq
3. Yup'ik

NORTHWEST COAST

1. Chinook
2. Haida
3. Lummi
4. Makah
5. Muckleshoot
6. Siletz
7. Skokomish
8. Tlingit
9. Tsimshian
10. Tulalip
11. Warm Springs

PLATEAU

1. Colville
2. Flathead
3. Nez Perce
4. Salish
5. Yakama

CALIFORNIA

1. Cahuilla
2. Hupa
3. Karuk
4. Mono Paiute
5. Pomo
6. Yokuts
7. Yurok

GREAT BASIN

1. Arapaho
2. Bannock
2a. Paiute
2b. Shoshone
3. Ute
4. Washoe

SOUTHWEST

1. Anasazi
2. Apache
2a. Chiricahua Apache
2b. Jicarilla Apache
2c. Mescalero Apache
2d. San Carlos Apache
2e. White Mountain Apache
3. Hopi
4. Hualapai
5. Navajo
6. Pueblos
6a. Acoma Pueblo
6b. Cochiti Pueblo
6c. Jemez Pueblo
6d. Laguna Pueblo
6e. San Ildefonso
6f. Santa Clara Pueblo
6g. Santo Domingo Pueblo
6h. Taos Pueblo
6i. Tesuque Pueblo
6j. Zia Pueblo
6k. Zuni Pueblo
7. Tohono O'odham
8. Yaqui

PLAINS

1. Assiniboine
2. Blackfeet (Piegan and Pikuni tribes)
3. Caddo
4. Cherokee
5. Cheyenne
6. Comanche
7. Crow
8. Fort Berthold Tribes
8a. Arikara
8b. Hidatsa
8c. Mandan
9. Kiowa
10. Omaha
11. Otoe
12. Pawnee
13. Ponca
14. Sac & Fox
15. Sioux
15a. Brule
15b. Lakota (Oglala)
15c. Standing Rock
15d. Yankton (Nakota)
16. Shawnee

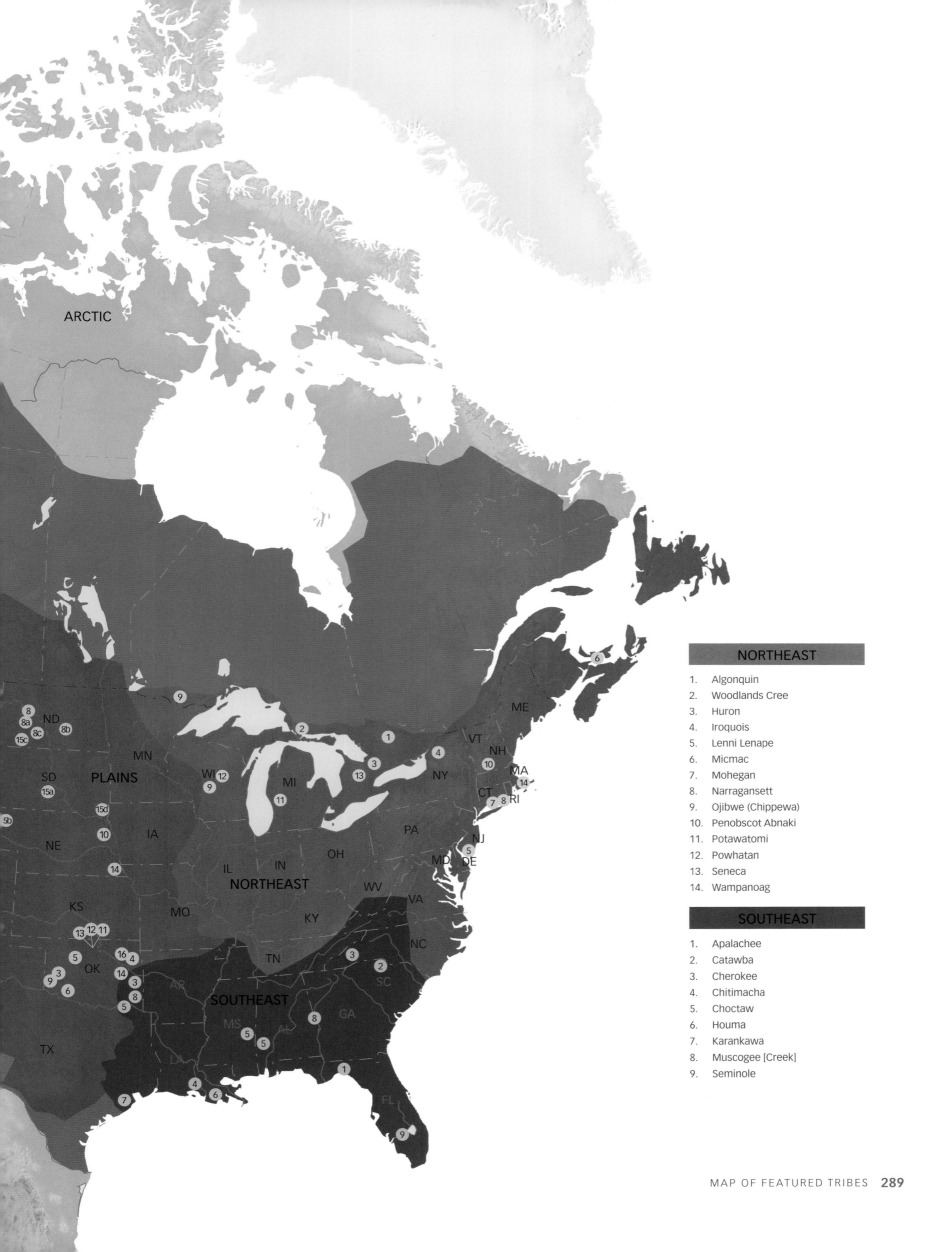

ARCTIC

ME
VT
NH
NY
MA
CT
RI
PA
NJ
OH
MD DE
WV
VA
KY
TN
NC
SC
GA
AL
MS
LA
FL

ND
MN
SD
WI
MI
IA
NE
IL
IN
KS
MO
OK
AR
TX

PLAINS

NORTHEAST

SOUTHEAST

Biographies

CONTRIBUTING AUTHORS

Dr. Bruce Bernstein is the Executive Director of the Southwestern Association for Indian Arts, the organization that organizes the renowned annual Santa Fe Indian Market. Previously, he was Assistant Director for collections and research at the Smithsonian's National Museum of the American Indian, as well as director of the Museum of Indian Arts and Culture in Santa Fe, New Mexico. He received his graduate and doctoral degrees from the University of New Mexico, and has written and curated broadly on Native arts.

Dr. George Charles is Director of the National Resource Center for American Indian, Alaska Native, and Native Hawaiian Elders at the University of Alaska, Anchorage. He is Yup'ik, and fluent in the Yupiaq language. He received his Ph.D. from the University of California, Santa Barbara, and has written extensively on Yupiaq and Native Alaskan languages, religious studies, and healing traditions. A US Navy Vietnam veteran, he credits his cultural perspectives to his Yup'ik elders.

Nephi Craig is Director of Native American Cuisine Studies at Classic Cooking Academy in Scottsdale, Arizona, responsible for researching and developing the first Native cuisine curriculum in the United States. A classically trained chef, he is also the founder of the Native American Culinary Association (NACA), a research and networking organization dedicated to the development and preservation of American Indian culinary traditions and professionals. Of Navajo and White Mountain Apache descent, he is a member of the White Mountain Apache tribe.

Emma Hansen is Curator of the Plains Indian Museum at the Buffalo Bill Historical Center in Cody, Wyoming. An enrolled member of the Pawnee Nation, her degrees include an M.A. in anthropology and an M.A. in sociology, both from the University of Oklahoma. She has curated several exhibitions and written extensively on Plains Indian arts and cultures, and has lectured at museums and universities in the United States, Canada, and Great Britain. Her most recent book is *Memory and Vision: Arts, Cultures, Histories, and Lives of Plains Indian People*.

Iris HeavyRunner-Pretty Paint is an educator, a researcher, and a leading authority on Native student retention and cultural resilience. She is Co-Director of ROSNA (Research Opportunities in Science for Native Americans) at the University of Montana, and in recognition of her dedication to the field, she was elected a member of the American Indian Graduate Center's Honorary Advisory Council of One Hundred Leaders, Scholars, and Traditionals. She is a member of the Blackfeet and Crow tribes. With her husband, Stan Pretty Paint, she began the Montana Indian Hall of Fame to honor influential Native song keepers.

Dr. Henrietta Mann, Cheyenne, holds a Ph.D. from the University of New Mexico, Albuquerque. She is Professor Emeritus in Native American Studies and Special Assistant to the President at Montana State University, Bozeman, and co-founded the Montana State University's Council of Elders, composed of leaders of all of Montana's tribes. On leave from MSU, she currently serves as President of the Cheyenne and Arapaho Tribal College, located on the campus of Southwestern Oklahoma State University in Weatherford.

Loretta Barrett Oden is a Citizen Band Potawatomi tribal member, and is an internationally recognized chef. Her five-part PBS series, *Seasoned with Spirit: A Native Cook's Journey*, won an Emmy in 2007. She has appeared on *Good Morning America, the Today Show,* and the TV Food Network, and was selected to serve on the board of directors of Chefs Collaborative. An active member of Slow Food International and Slow Food USA, she attended the Slow Food and Terre Madre Conference in Italy as a representative of the North American Indigenous Delegation. She also served as an expert reviewer for this work.

Dr. Janine Pease directs Native American Studies at Rocky Mountain College in Billings, Montana. For eighteen years, she served as president of Little Big Horn College in Crow Agency, Montana. She is a MacArthur Fellow, and was named National Indian Educator of the Year, as well as one of the fourteen most important American Indian leaders of the 20th century in *The New Warriors*. A woman of the Crow and Hidatsa tribes, Loves to Pray (her Crow Indian name) participates in sweat lodge ceremonies and gathers herbal foods and medicines for her family. Her publications focus on Plains Indian traditions, American Indian women's spiritual roles, education and language immersion schools, and voting rights.

EXPERT REVIEWERS

Dr. Rayna Green is Curator and Director of the American Indian Program at the National Museum of American History, Smithsonian Institution, and holds a Ph.D. in folklore and American studies. A member of the Cherokee Nation, she is a scholar, exhibition developer ("Julia Child's Kitchen" at the Smithsonian), filmmaker (*Corn Is Who We Are*), and writer. She specializes in American Indian history and culture and American/American Indian food and foodways.

Dr. Nancy Parezo holds a tenured Professorship in the University of Arizona's American Indian Studies department, as well as an appointment at the Arizona State Museum. She is also an affiliated Professor in Anthropology and a Research Associate for the Field Museum of Natural History. Her focus is on issues related to Southwest American Indian women's art production, and she has published extensively in the field.

Dr. Ken Pepion is Associate Vice President for Academic Affairs at Fort Lewis College in Durango, Colorado. He has held prior leadership positions at Harvard University, the Pacific Northwest National Laboratory, the Western Interstate Commission for Higher Education, the University of Arizona, Montana State University, and the University of Montana. In 2000, he received the Presidential Award for Excellence in Mathematics, Science, and Engineering Mentoring. He is a member of the Blackfeet tribe.

George Young has held a variety of positions in book publishing, including Editor-in-Chief at Ballantine Books, Vice President at Ten Speed Press, and Publisher of Comstock Editions, which specialized in books about the American West. He was the Executive Editor for *The Native Americans: An Illustrated History,* published in 1993.

Acknowledgments

NSAIE

The Knowledge Preservation Project is funded by a grant from the Administration for Native Americans (Grant No. 90-NA-7829), and addresses the goal of supporting local access to, control of, and coordination with, programs and services that safeguard the health, well-being and culture of Native peoples. The partnerships we have developed, the dedication of the NSAIE AmeriCorps VISTA members, and the support and funding we receive through the Administration for Native Americans and the Corporation for National and Community Service is making a positive difference for American Indian and Alaska Native elders at tribes throughout the United States. We have also been fortunate to work with the Title VI nutrition and Social Service Directors at Tribes and Tribal organizations across the United States.

The Corporation for National and Community Service, AmeriCorps VISTA (Volunteers in Service to America) members work at tribal sites through the National Society for American Indian Elderly's AmeriCorps VISTA project. These volunteers commit a year of full-time service to addressing issues of community and national importance. These dedicated individuals have our thanks and our admiration. The individuals we have encountered and worked with through various departments of the U.S. States, Health and Human Services and the Corporation for National Service exemplify the meaning of public service. Those listed in the acknowledgements quietly go about their work, making sure that Americans are served in part through community organizations such as ours.

Joyce McAfee, ACKO • Butch Artichoker, ACKO, Inc. • Billie Artichoker, ACKO, Inc. • Susan White, ACKO, Inc. • Christopher Beach, Administration for Native Americans • Michelle Fowler, Administration for Native Americans • Delia Carlyle, Chair Ak-Chin Indian Community, NSAIE Board Member • Quanah Crossland Stamps, Administration for Native Americans • John O'Brien, Administration for Native Americans • Oneida Winship, NSAIE Board Member • Lisa James, Cherokee Nation • Rebekah Willis, VISTA • Kimberly Will Broadie, CNCS Arizona Field Office • Ernesto Ramos, Former State Director, CNCS New Mexico Field Office • Michelle Griffith, CNCS • Kathie Ferguson-Avery, Corporation for National and Community Service • Lisa Guccione, Corporation for National and Community Service • Ken Hightower, Corporation for National and Community Service • Cathy Alvarez, Office of Grants Management • Laura Graham, VISTA • Mary Tenakhongva, Hopi tribe • Susan L. Washington, VISTA • Cynthia LaCounte, Turtle Mountain Chippewa • Robert Parisian • Dr. George Paul Charles, National Resource Center for American Indian, Alaska Native and Native Hawaiian Elders • Russell Maylone, Northwestern University • Samuel Fayuant, Tohono O'odham Pisinemo Recreation Center • Patricia Lucero, Pueblo of Isleta • Melissa Capoeman, Quinault Indian Nation • Pam James, Skokomish Tribal Nation • Rayna Green, Smithsonian Institute • Carmen Kalama, South Puget Indian Planning Agency • Melissa Christy, VISTA • Luella Harrison, Standing Rock Sioux • Victoria Collins, NSAIE • Jonathan Bougher, VISTA • Hilary McKinney, VISTA • Idaleen Reyes, Tohono O'odham Nation • Charla Nofire, NSAIE • Dollie J. Chauvin, NSAIE • Bernice Coker, U.S. Department of Health and Human Services, Office of Grants Management • Gordon James, Skokomish Tribal Nation • Brian King, ACKO, Inc. • Jayms Ramirez • Holly Staley • Arlo Starr, VISTA • Kathleen Telmont, ACKO, Inc. • Valerie Templin • Theron Wauneka, ACKO, Inc. • Steve Wilson, NSAIE Board Member • Twyla Baker-Demaray, UND/National Resource Center on Native American Aging • Dr. Leander "Russ" McDonald, UND/National Resource Center on Native American Aging • Kim Ruliffson, UND/National Resource Center on Native American Aging • Dr. Richard Ludtke, UND/National Resource Center on Native American Aging • Mary Gattis, UND/National Resource Center on Native American Aging • the former Dr. Alan Allery, UND/National Resource Center on Native American Aging • Dr. Yvonne Jackson, Director for American Indian, Alaska Native and Native Hawaiian Programs Administration on Aging • the former Tony Sanchez, former NSAIE Board Member • Syd Beane, former NSAIE Board Member • Tim Chapelle, U.S. Department of Health and Human Services, Administration for Children and Families, Office of Grants Management, Division of Discretionary Grants

WELDON OWEN

Weldon Owen would like to thank the staff at the National Museum of the American Indian's Cultural Resource Center for their help with collections and archival photography research, as well as those at the Institute of American Indian Arts, and the many galleries, museums, libraries, and nonprofits that contributed to this work. We would also like to extend our deepest gratitude to those tribes and tribal members who told us their stories and shared their experiences. Their commitment to accuracy lent a richness and depth to this project. Finally, we would like to thank the authors and experts for their enormous contributions to their chapters. It was an honor to work with them.

Fran Biehl, National Museum of the American Indian • Pat Nietfeld, National Museum of the American Indian • Lou Stancari, National Museum of the American Indian • Tatiana Slock, Institute of American Indian Arts • Paula Rivera, Institute of American Indian Arts • Glenn Linsenbardt, Fenimore Art Museum • Peter Stoessel, Blue Rain Gallery • Contessa Trujillo, Blue Rain Gallery • Jaime Lynn Gould, Medicine Man Gallery • Bill Soza • Anita Fields • Delbridge Honanie • Mateo Romero • Gary Crabbe • Jayms Ramirez • Mona Caron • Lee Marmon • Stephen Trimble • Clark Mishler • Natalie Fobes • Hope Richardson • Madeleine Adams • Rob James • Veronique Richardson • Ken Della Penta • Jen Straus • Alexa Hyman • Dan Goldberg • Eduardo Navarro • Alan Williams • Yvonne Fisher • Julien McRoberts • Ken Blackbird • Lois Ellen Frank • Brian Wignall • Sabra Moore • Kit Breen • James Marshall • Jack Storms • Mary Sage • John Bird • Allan Moss • Ruby Chimerica • Dale Carson • Michael Fitzgerald • Jake Hill • Butch Artichoker • Steven Foster • Anne McCudden • James Fortier, Turtle Island Productions • Freddie Lane, Lummi Nation • Walter Pacheco, Muckleshoot Nation • John Loftus • Gail Koffman • Tony Issacs, Indian House Records • Alex Alvarez • Cornelia Bowanie • Darrell Norman • Russell Standing Rock • Sidrick Baker and family • Stan PrettyPaint • Lieutenant Governor Pecos, Pueblo de Cochiti • David Boxley • Michael Horse • Norman Jackson • Roxanne Swentzell • Rebecca Bigwitch • Duane Maktima • Dan and Frances Namingha, Niman Gallery • DY Begay • Marcus Amerman • Marie Watt • A.J. Agard • John and Roby Littlefield, Dog Point Fish Camp • Pam and Gordon James • Hastings Shade • Terrol Dew Johnson, Tohono O'odham Community Action • Samuel Fayuant • Kirby Midori and family • America Meredith • Harold Littlebird

For Further Reading

Ballantine, Betty, and Ian Ballantine, eds. *The Native Americans*. Atlanta: Turner Publishing, Inc., 1993.

Berlo, Janet Catherine, and Ruth B. Phillips. *Native North American Art*. Oxford: Oxford University Press, 1998.

Bernstein, Bruce, and Gerald McMaster. *First American Art: The Charles and Valerie Diker Collection of American Indian Art*. Washington, D.C.: National Museum of the American Indian, Smithsonian Institution, in association with University of Washington Press, 2004.

Bonar, Eulalie H., ed. *Woven by the Grandmothers*. Washington, D.C.: Smithsonian Institution Press, 1996.

Champagne, Duane. *Native America: Portrait of the Peoples*. Canton, MI: Visible Ink Press, 1994.

Cichoke, Anthony J. *Secrets of Native American Herbal Remedies*. New York: Penguin Putnam Inc., 2001.

Cox, Beverly, and Martin Jacobs. *Spirit of the Harvest*. New York: Stewart, Tabori and Chang, 1991.
———. *Body, Mind, and Spirit: Native Cooking of the Americas*. Phoenix: Native Peoples, 2004.

D'Ambrosio, Paul, ed. *Heritage: The Magazine of the New York State Historical Association* 20 (2005).

Devon, Marjorie, ed. *Migrations: New Directions in Native American Art*. Albuquerque: University of New Mexico Press, 2006.

Dillingham, Rick. *Acoma and Laguna Pottery.* Santa Fe, NM: School of American Research Press, 1992.

Divina, Fernando, and Marlene Divina. *Foods of the Americas: Native Recipes and Traditions.* Berkeley, CA: Ten Speed Press, 2004.

Fauntleroy, Gussie. *Roxanne Swentzell: Extra Ordinary People.* Santa Fe: New Mexico Magazine, 2002.
———. "Tradition! Ancient Arts And Crafts Revived." *Native Peoples* XVIII, no. 6 (2005): 24–35.
———. "The Magic Flute: Timeless Native American Instrument." *Native Peoples* XIX, no. 6 (2006): 28–33.

Feest, Christian, ed. *The Cultures of Native North Americans*. Translated by Amanda Riddick, Sabine Troelsch, and Karen Waloschek. Cologne, Germany: Könemann Verlagsgesellschaft, 2000.

Fienup-Riordan, Ann, and others. *The Artists Behind The Work*. Fairbanks: University of Alaska Museum, 1986.

Greene, Jacqueline D. *The Tohono O'odham.* New York: Franklin Watts, 1998.

Harlow, Francis H. *Two Hundred Years of Historic Pueblo Pottery: The Gallegos Collection.* Santa Fe, NM: Morning Star Gallery, 1990.

Harris, Lorie K. *Tlingit Tales.* Happy Camp, CA: Naturegraph Publishers, Inc., 1985.

Her Many Horses, Emil, ed. *Identity by Design*. Washington, D.C.: Smithsonian Institution, 2007.

Heth, Charlotte, ed. *Native American Dance: Ceremonies and Social Traditions.* Washington, D.C.: National Museum of the American Indian, Smithsonian Institution, with Starwood Publishing, Inc., 1992.

Hill, Tom, and Richard Hill, Sr., eds. *Creation's Journey.* Washington, D.C.: Smithsonian Institution Press, 1994.

Hooker, Kathy Eckles. *Time Among the Navajo.* Santa Fe: Museum of New Mexico Press, 1991.

Hutchens, Alma R. *Indian Herbalogy of North America.* Boston: Shambhala Publications, Inc., 1973.

Iverson, Peter. *Diné: A History of the Navajos.* Albuquerque: University of New Mexico Press, 2002.

Johnson, Tim, ed. *Spirit Capture.* Washington, D.C.: Smithsonian Institution Press, 1998.

Joseph, Robert, ed. *Listening to Our Ancestors.* Washington, D.C.: National Geographic Society, 2005.

Josephy, Alvin M., Jr. *500 Nations: An Illustrated History of North American Indians.* New York: Gramercy Books, 1994.

Kaiper, Dan, and Nan Kaiper. *Tlingit: Their Art, Culture and Legends.* Seattle: Hancock House Publishers, Inc., 1978.

Kavasch, E. Barrie. *Enduring Harvests.* Lincoln, Nebraska: Globe Pequot Press, 1995.
———. *Native Harvests.* Mineola, NY: Dover Publications, Inc., 2005.

Kosh, A. M. *Alaska Native Cultures.* Edited by Angela Tripp. Santa Barbara, CA: Albion Publishing Group, 1994.

Lowie, Robert H. *Indians of the Plains.* Reprint, with a preface by Raymond J. DeMallie. Lincoln: University of Nebraska Press, 1982.

McLaughlin, Castle. *Arts of Diplomacy.* Seattle: University of Washington Press, 2003.

McMaster, Gerald, and Clifford E. Trafzer, eds. *Native Universe.* Washington, D.C.: National Geographic Society, 2004.

Matuz, Roger, ed. *St. James Guide to Native North American Artists.* Detroit: St. James Press, 1998.

National Museum of the American Indian. *Born of Clay: Ceramics from the National Museum of the American Indian.* Washington, D.C.: Smithsonian Institution, 2005.

Payton, Colleen M. "Traditional Native Dance, Past and Present." *Native Peoples* XIX, no. 5 (2006): 46–51.

Peterson, Susan. *The Living Tradition of Maria Martinez.* New York: Kodansha International, 1977.

Pritzker, Barry M. *A Native American Encyclopedia.* New York: Oxford University Press, 2000.

Rushing, W. Jackson III, ed. *Native American Art in the Twentieth Century.* New York: Routledge, 1999.

Schaaf, Gregory. *Hopi-Tewa Pottery: 500 Artist Biographies.* Santa Fe, NM: CIAC Press, 1998.

Swentzell, Rina. "Accommodating the World: Cultural Tourism Among the Pueblos." *Awek:kon Journal* XI (Fall/Winter 1994): 134–138.

Taylor, Colin, ed. *The Native Americans.* San Diego, CA: Thunder Bay Press, 1991.

Thornton, L. F. "Weaving Through Time." *New Mexico Magazine* 58, no. 8 (2007): 52–55.

Tooker, Elisabeth, ed. *Native North American Spirituality of the Eastern Woodlands.* New York: Paulist Press, 1979.

Vincent, Gilbert T., Sherry Brydon, and Ralph T. Coe, eds. *Art of the North American Indians: The Thaw Collection.* Seattle: University of Washington Press, 2000.

Waldman, Carl. *Atlas of the North American Indian.* New York: Checkmark Books, 2000.

Walker, Richard. "Potlatch: Profound Ceremony and Celebration, Northwest Coast Style." *Native Peoples* XX, no. 6 (2007): 28–35.

Wyckoff, Lydia L., ed. *Woven Worlds: Basketry from the Clark Field Collection.* Tulsa, OK: The Philbrook Museum of Art: 2001.

Yellowtail, Thomas. *Native Spirit: The Sun Dance Way.* Bloomington, IN: World Wisdom, Inc., 2007.

www.bbhc.org/pointswest/index.cfm
*Online archive for *Points West,* the quarterly journal of the Buffalo Bill Historical Center and the Plains Indian Museum

www.nmai.si.edu
*Official website of the Smithsonian's National Museum of the American Indian

www.iaia.edu/museum
*Official website of the Institute of American Indian Arts Museum

www.alaskanative.net
*Official website of the Alaska Native Heritage Center in Anchorage

www.tocaonline.org/homepage.html
*Official website of the nonprofit Tohono O'odham Community Action

Art and Photography Credits

Unless otherwise indicated, images are listed from upper left-hand corner to lower right-hand corner.

Abbreviations
National Museum of the American Indian (NMAI)
Institute for American Indian Arts (IAIA)

Cover
Front: Courtesy of IAIA; **Back:** Courtesy of NMAI, Smithsonian Institution.

Front Matter
1–2: NMAI, Smithsonian Institution, photo by Dan Goldberg, 2007; courtesy of the NMAI, Smithsonian Institution. **2–3:** artwork courtesy of Blue Rain Gallery, Santa Fe, New Mexico. **4–5:** photo P11433 courtesy of NMAI, Smithsonian Institution. **6–7:** photo by Alan Williams, 2007. **8–9:** photos by Sidrick Baker, Jim Marshall, Alan Williams, Jayms Ramirez, Stephen Trimble, Lois Ellen Frank, and Kit Breen. **10–11:** Corbis NA005722. **12–13:** Illustrations courtesy of Mona Caron.

Chapter 1
14–15: artwork courtesy of Malcolm Furlow. **18–19:** NMAI, Smithsonian Institution; artwork courtesy of Sabra Moore, 1998; Carrie M. McLain Memorial Museum/Alaskastock.com, 2007. **20–21:** photo N12398 courtesy of NMAI, Smithsonian Institution; photo by Richard Walker, Thaw Collection, Fenimore Art Museum, Cooperstown, New York. **22–23:** Marilyn Angel Wynn/Nativestock.com; Milton Snow/Corbis, 1941; photo by Dan Goldberg, 2007; Richard Cummins/Corbis; Solus/Veer. **24–25:** photos by Natalie Fobes. **26–27:** NMAI, Smithsonian Institution, photos by Dan Goldberg, 2007; National Anthropological Archives. **28–29:** photos by Stephen Trimble; photo P11433 courtesy of NMAI, Smithsonian Institution. **30–31:** photo by Clark Mishler; photo by Roy M. Corral, 2007. **32–33:** Asahel Curtis/Corbis, 1920; NMAI, Smithsonian Institution, photo by Dan Goldberg, 2007; photo by Ken Blackbird; McCormick Library of Special Collections, NorthWestern University Library.

Chapter 2
34–35: artwork courtesy of IAIA. **38–39:** Illustrations courtesy of Brian Wignall, 2008; Corbis NA005722. **40–41:** NMAI, Smithsonian Institution, photo by Dan Goldberg, 2007; courtesy of NMAI, Smithsonian Institution; NMAI, Smithsonian Institution, photo by Dan Goldberg, 2007. **42–43:** photo courtesy of Michael Berman. **44–45:** Mimotto Digital Visions/Getty; photo by Dan Goldberg, 2007; food styling by Jen Straus. **46–47:** NMAI, Smithsonian Institution, photos by Dan Goldberg, 2007; photos by John Bigelow Taylor, Thaw Collection, Fenimore Art Museum, Cooperstown, New York. **48–49:** NMAI, Smithsonian Institution, photos by Dan Goldberg, 2007. **50–51:** photo by Dan Goldberg, 2007; food styling by Jen Straus; Scott T. Smith/Corbis; photos by Stephen Trimble. **52–53:** Minnesota Historical Society N1903; photo courtesy of Allan Moss, 2006; Minnesota Historical Society N92704; Milwaukee Public Museum N5780. **54–55:** artwork courtesy of IAIA. **56–57:** Brand X/Veer; photo by Dan Goldberg, 2007; food styling by Jen Straus; Ryan/Beyer Stone/Getty; photo by Dan Goldberg, 2007. **58–59:** photos by Lois Ellen Frank; McCormick Library of Special Collections, NorthWestern University Library. **60–61:** photos by Clark Mishler. **62–63:** photo by Steven Foster; Bernard Dupont/Alamy; Steve Terill/Corbis, 2002; photo by Dan Goldberg, 2007; food styling by Jen Straus. **64–65:** Corbis, 1894; Darlyne A. Murawski, National Geographic/Getty; photo by Jayms Ramirez, 2007; Nicholas Lemonnier,

Stock Food Creative/Getty. **66–67:** Palace of the Governors Photo Archives N042075; NMAI, Smithsonian Institution, photos by Dan Goldberg, 2007. **68–69:** NMAI, Smithsonian Institution, photos by Dan Goldberg, 2007. **70–71:** photo by Dan Goldberg, 2007; food styling by Jen Straus; Pat and Chuck Blackley/AGPix.com; Preston Schlebusch, The Image Bank/Getty; Darrell Gulin/Corbis. **72–73:** Marilyn Angel Wynn/Nativestock.com; photo by Jayms Ramirez, 2007. **74–75:** photo by Dan Goldberg, 2007; food styling by Jen Straus; Swift/Corbis; photo by Dan Goldberg, 2007. **76–77:** photo by Lois Ellen Frank; photo by John Elk III; age fotostock/Veer; Bob Sacha/Corbis. **78–79:** Panoramic Images/Getty; photo by Dan Goldberg, 2007; food styling by Jen Straus; Karl Kinne, zefa/Corbis; photo by Dan Goldberg, 2007. **80–81:** Minnesota Historical Society N4995A; Minnesota Historical Society N5000A; Minnesota Historical Society N35312; Johannes Kroemer, Photonica/Getty. **82–83:** photo by Dan Goldberg, 2007; food styling by Jen Straus; Pat O'Hara/Corbis; Minnesota Historical Society N92704. **84–85:** photo by Clark Mishler; photo by Jayms Ramirez, 2007; Carr Clifton, Minden Pictures/Getty.

Chapter 3
86–87: artwork courtesy of Blue Rain Gallery, Santa Fe, New Mexico. **90–91:** McCormick Library of Special Collections, NorthWestern University Library; artwork courtesy of Sabra Moore, 1998. **92–93:** artwork courtesy of Sabra Moore, 1998; artwork courtesy of Blue Rain Gallery, Santa Fe, New Mexico. **94–95:** Yakima Valley Library N2002-851-196; photos by Steven Foster; Jurgen Vogt/Getty. **96–97:** photo by Jayms Ramirez, 2007; photos by Steven Foster; Ira Block/National Geographic. **98–99:** NMAI, Smithsonian Institution, photos by Dan Goldberg, 2007; second-from-left pipe bag courtesy of NMAI, Smithsonian Institution. **100–101:** photo by Jayms Ramirez, 2007; Panoramic Images/Getty; photo by Richard Throssel, University of Wyoming Heritage Center TP149. **102–103:** photo P18096 courtesy of NMAI, Smithsonian Institution; courtesy of NMAI, Smithsonian Institution; Philbrook Museum of Art, Inc., Tulsa, Oklahoma. **104–105:** courtesy of NMAI, Smithsonian Institution. **106–107:** artwork courtesy of Blue Rain Gallery, Santa Fe, New Mexico. **108–109:** George H. H. Huey; photo by Jayms Ramirez, 2007; photo N24484 courtesy of NMAI, Smithsonian Institution. **110–111:** photos courtesy of Michael Fitzgerald from Native Spirit: The Sun Dance Way. **112–113:** Werner Forman/Corbis; artwork courtesy of The Bridgeman Art Library, Stapleton Collection. **114–115:** NMAI, Smithsonian Institution, photo by Dan Goldberg, 2007; courtesy of NMAI, Smithsonian Institution. **116–117:** photo by Joe Sohm. **118–119:** artwork courtesy of the Collection of the Manitoba Arts Council, 1988; photo by John Bigelow Taylor, Thaw Collection, Fenimore Art Museum, Cooperstown, New York; NMAI, Smithsonian Institution, photos by Dan Goldberg, 2007. **120–121:** photo by Tom Melham/National Geographic Images.

Chapter 4
122–123: artwork courtesy of Blue Rain Gallery, Santa Fe, New Mexico. **126–127:** illustrations courtesy of Brian Wignall, 2008; artwork courtesy of IAIA. **128–129:** McCormick Library of Special Collections, NorthWestern University Library; artwork courtesy of del Rio Gallery. **130–131:** Ira Block/National Geographic; photo by John Bigelow Taylor, Thaw Collection, Fenimore Art Museum, Cooperstown, New York; Richard A. Cooke/Corbis, 1986. **132–133:** Marilyn Angel Wynn/Nativestock.com; NMAI, Smithsonian Institution, photo by Dan Goldberg, 2007. **134–135:** photos courtesy of Jack Storms, 2007. **136–137:** Altrendo Panoramic; photo courtesy of James Fortier,

Turtle Island Productions, 2006. **138–139:** images by Marilyn Angel Wynn/ Nativestock.com. **140–141:** photos by Richard Walker and John Bigelow Taylor, Thaw Collection, Fenimore Art Museum, Cooperstown, New York.

Chapter 5
142–143: artwork courtesy of NMAI, Smithsonian Institution. **146–147:** photo courtesy of Sidrick Baker; illustrations courtesy of Brian Wignall, 2008. **148–149:** photos by Kit Breen; Thaw Collection, Fenimore Art Museum, Cooperstown, New York. **150–151:** photos by Alan Williams, 2007. **152–153:** photos by Alan Williams, 2007. **154–155:** NMAI, Smithsonian Institution, photos by Dan Goldberg, 2007; Corbis NA012353. **156–157:** photo by John Bigelow Taylor, Thaw Collection, Fenimore Art Museum, Cooperstown, New York; NMAI, Smithsonian Institution, photos by Dan Goldberg, 2007. **158–159:** NMAI, Smithsonian Institution, photo by Dan Goldberg, 2007; courtesy of NMAI, Smithsonian Institution; photo courtesy of Frashers Fotos Collection, 1936. **160–161:** artwork courtesy of Lee Marmon, 1962. **162–163:** Marilyn Angel Wynn/Nativestock.com; photo by John C. H. Grabill, Smithsonian Institution/Corbis, 1890; Private Collection, The Bridgeman Art Library, Stapleton Collection. **164–165:** photos courtesy of Sidrick Baker; photo courtesy of Tony Issacs, Indian House Records. **166–167:** photo by Gary Crabbe / Enlightened Images. **168–169:** photos by Alan Williams, 2007. **170–171:** photos by Alan Williams, 2007. **172–173:** photos by John Bigelow Taylor, Thaw Collection, Fenimore Art Museum, Cooperstown, New York; NMAI, Smithsonian Institution, photo by Dan Goldberg, 2007; photo by John Bigelow Taylor, Thaw Collection, Fenimore Art Museum, Cooperstown, New York. **174–175:** photo by John Bigelow Taylor, Thaw Collection, Fenimore Art Museum, Cooperstown, New York; NMAI, Smithsonian Institution, photos by Dan Goldberg, 2007. **176–177:** photos by Alan Williams, 2007.

Chapter 6
178–179: artwork courtesy of Norman Jackson. **182–183:** illustration courtesy of Brian Wignall, 2008; California Historical Society, 1900; Yosemite Research Library, National Park Service, 1933. **184–185:** photo by Hobart Edwards, courtesy of Medicine Man Gallery, Santa Fe, New Mexico; NMAI, Smithsonian Institution, photo by Dan Goldberg, 2007. **186–187:** Medicine Man Gallery, Santa Fe, New Mexico; photo by Adamson Clark Vroman, courtesy of the Southwest Museum Collection, Los Angeles; Medicine Man Gallery, Santa Fe, New Mexico. **188–189:** photo courtesy of NMAI, Smithsonian Institution; NMAI, Smithsonian Institution, photos by Dan Goldberg, 2007. **190–191:** photo courtesy of Roxanne Swentzell; photo by Julien McRoberts; photo courtesy of Roxanne Swentzell. **192–193:** artwork courtesy of Niman Gallery; photo by Adamson Clark Vroman, courtesy of the Southwest Museum Collection, Los Angeles; photo by Eric Swanson; photo by Richard Walker, Thaw Collection, Fenimore Art Museum, Cooperstown, New York. **194–195:** Pat O'Hara/Corbis, 1989; Danny Lehman/Corbis, 2000; Corbis; Vince Streano/Corbis, 1988. **196–197:** Altrendo Images; Tom Bean/Corbis, 1986; Tim Thompson/Corbis, 1992. **198–199:** photos by Clark Mishler; Blue Rain Gallery, Santa Fe, New Mexico; photo by Russel Johnson. **200–201:** photo by John Bigelow Taylor, Thaw Collection, Fenimore Art Museum, Cooperstown, New York. **202–203:** photo by John Bigelow Taylor, Thaw Collection, Fenimore Art Museum, Cooperstown, New York; courtesy of NMAI, Smithsonian Institution; courtesy of Gathering Tribes Gallery, Oakland, California. **204–205:** Images Etc. Limited. **206–207:** artwork courtesy of

IAIA; courtesy of NMAI, Smithsonian Institution. **208–209:** courtesy of NMAI, Smithsonian Institution; photos by John Bigelow Taylor and Richard Walker, Thaw Collection, Fenimore Art Museum, Cooperstown, New York. **210–211:** photos by Alan Williams, 2007. **212–213:** NMAI, Smithsonian Institution, photos by Dan Goldberg, 2007.

Chapter 7
214–215: artwork courtesy of D.Y. Begay. **218–219:** photo N13620 courtesy of NMAI, Smithsonian Institution; National Anthropological Archives. **220–221:** illustrations courtesy of Brian Wignall, 2008; photo by John Bigelow Taylor, Thaw Collection, Fenimore Art Museum, Cooperstown, New York. **222–223:** NMAI, Smithsonian Institution, photos by Dan Goldberg, 2007. **224–225:** photos courtesy of Marcus Amerman. **226–227:** NMAI, Smithsonian Institution, photos by Dan Goldberg, 2007. **228–229:** photo by John Bigelow Taylor, Thaw Collection, Fenimore Art Museum, Cooperstown, New York; Nebraska State Historical Society RG2969.PH:2-1. **230–231:** NMAI, Smithsonian Institution, photos by Dan Goldberg, 2007. **232–233:** photos courtesy of Marie Watt. **234–235:** Denver Public Library X-33039; NMAI, Smithsonian Institution, photo by Dan Goldberg, 2007; photos by Julien McRoberts, 2007. **236–237:** photo by John Bigelow Taylor, Thaw Collection, Fenimore Art Museum, Cooperstown, New York; NMAI, Smithsonian Institution, photos by Dan Goldberg, 2007. **238–239:** Denver Public Library X-33042; courtesy of NMAI, Smithsonian Institution. **240–241:** courtesy of NMAI, Smithsonian Institution. **242–243:** photos by Jim Marshall, 2007. **244–245:** photos by Alan Williams, 2007; NMAI, Smithsonian Institution, photo by Dan Goldberg, 2007. **246–247:** NMAI, Smithsonian Institution, photo by Dan Goldberg, 2007; Marilyn Angel Wynn/ Nativestock.com. **248–249:** photo by B.B. Dobbs, University of Alaska Fairbanks; photo by Ethel Ross Oliver, University of Alaska Fairbanks; photo by John Bigelow Taylor, Thaw Collection, Fenimore Art Museum, Cooperstown, New York.

Chapter 8
250–251: artwork courtesy of IAIA. **254–255:** Alaska State Library Collection ASL-P306-0581; Alaska State Library Collection ASL-P306-0407; artwork courtesy of Nick Charles and the University of Alaska Museum. **256–257:** photo courtesy of Dr. George Charles; courtesy of NMAI, Smithsonian Institution. **258–259:** photo courtesy of NMAI, Smithsonian Institution; photo P03706 courtesy of NMAI, Smithsonian Institution; photo by Richard Throssel, courtesy of University of Wyoming's American Heritage Center; courtesy of University of Nevada–Reno Library. **260–261:** photos by Jayms Ramirez, 2007. **262–263:** photos by Jayms Ramirez, 2007. **264–265:** photos by Jayms Ramirez, 2007; NMAI, Smithsonian Institution, photo by Dan Goldberg, 2007. **266–267:** artwork courtesy of America Meredith. **268–269:** photo by Russell Lee/Getty Images; photo by Kit Breen; Getty Images, 2004; Harald Sun/Getty Images. **270–271:** courtesy of NMAI, Smithsonian Institution. **272–273:** photos by Kit Breen. **274–275:** photo by Jan Lucie; photo by Kit Breen. **276–277:** photos by Jayms Ramirez, 2007; artwork courtesy of Philbrook Museum of Art, Inc., Tulsa, Oklahoma; NMAI, Smithsonian Institution, photo by Dan Goldberg, 2007. **278–285:** photos by Jayms Ramirez, 2007.

Back Matter
286–287: artwork courtesy of IAIA. **288–289:** illustration courtesy of Adrienne Aquino and Map Resources. **292–293:** photo by John Bigelow Taylor, Thaw Collection, Fenimore Museum, Cooperstown, New York. **302–303:** photo by Kit Breen.

Index

A

Abeyta, Tony, 88
Acoma, 43
Acorns, 18, 40
Adams, Gladys and DeForest, 155
Agard, A. J., 275
Aged Tutor and Young Students
    (Begay), 277
Algonquin, 70, 182
Amerman, Marcus, 220, 224–25
Amiotte, Arthur, 201
Anasazi
    basketmaking, 204–5
    buildings, 204–5
    irrigation systems, 28
    jewelry, 237
    petroglyphs, 91
    pottery, 188, 205
Animals
    as emblems, 118
    power of, 13, 119
Annedda, 89
Apache, 19, 43, 150–51, 156
Apalachee, 38
Architecture, 268, 271
Arikara, 40, 90, 165, 218
Arlee, Johnny, 148
Arnica, 89
Art and craft
    See also individual crafts
    emerging mediums in,
        206–7
    functionality and, 181
    innovation and, 181
    popularity of, among
        non-Natives, 182
    significance of, 181,
        182–84, 198
Artichoker, Butch, 100
Assiniboine, 231
Ayaginar, 255

B

Baker, Bill, 146, 165
Baker, Sidrick, 164
Balsam root, 89
Bannock, 32–33

Baranof Island, 278–79
Basketmaking, 27, 40,
    66, 182, 184, 208–9,
    211–12, 260–64
Beacon Lights (Keyser), 209
Beading, 218–20, 224–25, 226, 231
The Beadmaker (Amerman), 224
Beans
    as part of the Three Sisters,
        22, 78
    Three Sisters Sauté with
        Sage Pesto, 50
    varieties of, 23
Beargrass, 260, 264
Bear's Lodge, 101
Beaver, Fred, 139
Beaver, Vance, 272w
Begay, D. Y., 216, 242
Begay, Harrison, 277
Bella Bella, 69
Ben, Joe, Jr., 107
Benedict, Florence
    Katsitsienhawi, 209
Bentwood boxes, 69
Berries, 84, 126
Bigfoot, 162
Bighorn Medicine Wheel, 120
Bigwind, Mary, 80
Bigwitch, Rebecca, 211
Birchbark biting, 182
Bird, John, 71
Bison
    See Buffalo
Black cohosh, 89
Blackfeet, 71, 114, 226
Black Hawk, Chief, 201, 202
Blankets, 105, 232–33, 239,
    241, 245
Blanket strips, 231
Blowguns, 20
Bonnemaison, Fereol, 162
Bow and Arrow Diptych (Furlow), 14
Bowannie, Cornelia, 176
Boxley, David, 169, 170, 171
Braid (Watt), 232
Brown, Steve, 197
Buffalo (bison), 17, 18, 20,
    32–33, 128
    Spice-Rubbed American
        Bison Tenderloin, 45
Buffalo Dance, 155

Busk, 139
Buttons, 245

C

Cahuilla, 182
Calamint, 96
Cannon, T. C., 206
Canoes, 134
Catawba, 20
Cattle, 71
Cedar, 89, 95
Celestine, Molly, 260
Charles, Nick, 255
Cherokee, 27, 174, 211, 267
Cheyenne
    beading, 219
    dances, 173
    musical instruments, 147, 156
    quillwork, 218
    Water Prayer, 125
Chiles, 76–77
Chilkat, 247
Chippewa, 53, 126, 146
Chitimacha, 38, 66, 116–17
Choctaw, 38, 66
Clambakes, 65
Clothing, 173–74, 217–20,
    245, 247–49, 256
Cochiti, 159
Comanche, 219
Concho belts, 234
Cooking
    See Foodways; Recipes, Corn
    as part of the Three Sisters,
        22, 78
    significance of, 125
Corn Dance, 127–28, 130–31
Corn Dancers (Roybal), 127
Corn People of the Four Directions
    (Lomakema), 128
Cornhusk bags, 47–48
Cox, Debra, 220
Cranberries, 71
    Turkey with Cranberry-Piñon
        Sauce, 70
Creation stories, 55, 92, 102,
    114, 116–17, 253, 271
Cree, 162, 167, 182
Creek, 152, 167